COPING

AS A

Survivor of

Violent Crime

Barbara Moe

THE ROSEN PUBLISHING GROUP, INC./NEW YORK

Published in 1995 by The Rosen Publishing Group, Inc.
29 East 21st Street, New York, NY 10010

First Edition

Library of Congress Cataloging-in-Publication

Moe, Barbara.
    Coping when you are a survivor of a violent crime / Barbara
Moe.—1st ed.
    Includes bibliographical references and index.
    ISBN 0-8239-1882-3
    1. Youth—Crimes against—United States—Case studies—
Juvenile literature. 2. Victims of crimes—United States—Case
studies—Juvenile literature. 3. Violent crimes—United States—Case
studies—Juvenile literature. [1. Victims of crimes. 2. Violent
crimes.] I. Title.
    HV6250.4.Y68M64 1994
    362.88—dc20   94-14117
                                                                CIP
                                                                AC

Manufactured in the United States of America

ABOUT THE AUTHOR ◇

Barbara Moe has a Bachelor of Science degree in Nursing from the College of Nursing and Health, University of Cincinnati, and a Master of Science degree in Nursing from Ohio State University. She received a Master of Social Work degree, as well as a certificate in Marriage and Family Therapy, from the University of Denver.

Author's Note: All of the scenarios in this book are true. Some come directly from the persons affected by the violent crimes. Others come from newspaper and magazine accounts. Most of those telling their stories are high school students who responded to a questionnaire and participated in interviews. Only their names and certain circumstances have been changed.

Contents

CHAPTER 1

The Big Picture

This book has three purposes: (1) to help survivors of crime learn to cope with past experiences and get on with their lives; (2) to help all young people avoid becoming victims; and (3) to encourage nonviolent ways of solving conflicts. Through explanations, stories, and suggestions, we will look at crime from many different perspectives.

WHAT IS CRIME?

Every day in the United States approximately 16,000 violent crimes are committed or attempted. The dictionary defines crime as any "unlawful act." Liz Loescher, executive director of the Conflict Center in Denver, Colorado, defines violence as "anything that hurts another."

"So what else is new?" you say. "I read the papers and watch the news every day. People are always doing unlawful acts and harming each other."

Morton Bard and Dawn Sangrey in *The Crime Victim's Book* stress the pain crime inflicts on any victim. "Every victim of a personal crime is confronted with a brutal reality: the deliberate violation of one human being by another." No matter what the crime, they write, "the essential injury is the same. Victims have been assaulted—emotionally and sometimes physically—by a predator who has shaken their world to its foundations." A violent crime destroys two essential beliefs: the victim's sense of trust and sense of control over his or her life.

Not all violence is considered a crime, nor is all crime violent. Say, for example, you are standing in line at McDonald's. Someone pushes you out of your place in line. Most young people say they had no idea pushing was a crime. But pushing and shoving are considered third-degree assault. Usually the police and courts are busy with more serious matters, but if you punch the pushy person in the mouth or threaten him with a weapon, the police may come.

Dennis Kennedy is executive director of Project PAVE (Promoting Alternatives to Violence through Education). When Kennedy travels to schools to talk about his program, he goes over definitions of the various forms of violence. Violence, he says, is a harmful and intentional crossing of boundaries. This kind of abuse hurts a person's body, his feelings, or both. Abuse has many forms:

Physical: Any action that hurts another's body. Hitting, pinching, kicking, spitting, and beating are all forms of physical abuse. Neglect of a child is also abuse.

Sexual: Any kind of sexual interaction that makes a person uncomfortable and is against that person's will. This form of abuse includes sexual harassment (verbal or physical), rape, and incest.

Emotional: Anything that hurts another's feelings

or makes fun of his or her feelings. Emotional abuse includes put-downs, name-calling, sarcasm, mean looks, and exclusion of someone from a group.

What is the risk of becoming the victim of a violent crime? According to *Understanding and Preventing Violence*, the annual risk of becoming a victim of personal violence in 1990 was 1 in 34 for those over the age of twelve. The risk of becoming a victim of personal theft was 1 in 16. FBI statistics show that figures have risen in recent years in every important category of crime except burglary. Statistics for robbery and car theft show the greatest increase, but the numbers of homicides and rapes have increased at an alarming rate.

All victims feel violated in some way. They struggle with feelings of fear and anger, guilt and shame. Maria, whose friend died in a gang homicide, says, "I felt terrible. I had a guilty feeling. I kind of think it was my fault. I shouldn't have joined that gang and brought him into it."

Kathleen, a rape victim, says her immediate reaction was one of confusion. "At first I wasn't sure what had happened." Later she found herself avoiding anyone who resembled the person who raped her. She searched to find something positive about what had happened. Finally she said, "That I survived."

The victim of a burglary, Ben, was only ten years old when someone broke into his home. At first he felt "disbelief." The break-in, which occurred at night, seemed like a nightmare from which he hoped soon to wake. Later he was afraid to go into the living room at night. He did have one positive reaction. He felt overwhelming gratitude to his dogs that had chased away the burglar.

Two other victims, Cal and Laura, could find nothing

positive about what happened to them. Cal, who woke up to find the family's van of furniture stolen, says he exploded with anger. Later he felt distrust of the people in his neighborhood. Laura's aunt suffered the violent act of a purse-snatching. Laura, who hadn't even experienced the crime, felt fear. Walking anywhere alone gave her the jitters. She never again walked in an alley.

If you think these young people are describing isolated incidents, consider the following:

- The rate of serious assault in Chicago increased by 400 percent between 1974 and 1991.
- Violence is the leading cause of death for people between the ages of 15 and 34 years.
- Bureau of Justice statistics estimate that 83 percent of those currently age 12 will be violently victimized in their lifetime.
- Approximately half of all homicides are committed by someone known to the victim—friends, neighbors, associates in illegal activities, members of a rival gang or their own gang, casual acquaintances, or someone from work.
- People between the ages of 12 and 24 have the highest of all victimization rates in crimes of violence and theft.

According to some authorities, we are all victims of crime because we all *fear* victimization. If the victim is a friend, we may avoid that person because what happened to him is a reminder of what could happen to us. This withdrawal of support causes the survivor of a violent crime to feel even more isolated.

Victims need to know that they are not alone, that they are *not* crazy. Their feelings are normal. They need support from family and friends, they need to know what to expect from the police and the court system, and they need to know where else to look for help.

Rape victim Maria found support in "lots of good friends" and in her own inner strength. At times she still gets depressed. "I'm in a therapy group," says Maria, "and the other girls in the group really help." She gives this advice to those who have experienced similar violence: "Seek help. Get some kind of therapy. Don't let anyone tell you how you should feel."

Laura, who learned a great deal from her aunt's experience with a purse-snatcher, says, "Be aware, never walk alone, and always be ready to protect yourself." Laura and her aunt found support in family cooperation. "We called a meeting, got together and talked, and since then we've all worked as a team to help each other."

These few examples show *what* crime is. The next chapter discusses the *whys* of crime and criminal behavior.

CHAPTER 2

Why Does Violent Crime Exist?

No one fully understands the increase of violence in our society. Dr. Kenneth Powell of the Centers for Disease Control and Prevention in Atlanta suggests some possible causes for the "disease" of crime. They include poverty, the easy availability of drugs and alcohol, media images, and the attitudes of society.

Add guns to the list. Although firearms do not always create the problem, they make the outcome more serious, and often fatal, for the victim. Guns are killing teens at the highest rate ever; they are now responsible for more teenage deaths than all natural diseases combined. In 1990 guns killed 4,173 young people ages 14 to 19. That's eleven a day, an increase of about 77 percent in five years. A recent report from the Justice Department estimates that 100,000 children carry guns to school every day.

What about kids who kill? Who are these children and why do they kill? We have many guesses but no solid answers. A combination of factors is the best guess. Gary Rummler of the *Milwaukee Journal* says, "These children are a complex mix of fear, anger and turmoil, plus a deadly sense of pride, an appalling ignorance about alternative approaches to solving problems, and a distorted sense of ownership, not to mention the guns." It's interesting, observes Rummler, that some of the kids pulling the triggers are poor, but some are rich. Some come from violent homes, but some do not. Some have only one parent, but some have two. Experts in ethics and morality say that not enough effort is going into teaching young people the importance of being considerate of others.

Thomas Grundle, a clinical psychologist at the Milwaukee County Child and Adolescent Treatment Center, says that many families don't teach problem-solving. In addition, children don't learn to deal with frustration. Many expect instant gratification. Add to such a person low self-esteem, no hope for the future, and a gun in his hand. What do you have? Trouble.

FINDING A CURE

If the causes of crime are so complicated, how can we find a cure? Experts have found it helpful to think of crime as a disease or as a public health problem. Some compare finding a cure for violent crime with finding a cure for cancer. Just as there are many kinds of cancer, there are many kinds of violent crime.

Possible cures for the disease of violence include teaching nonviolent ways of settling disputes, making mentors available, and providing parenting classes, job programs, structured recreation and sports, and other special opportunities to change the environment for young people.

Deborah Prothrow-Stith, M.D., is the author of *Deadly*

Consequences: How Violence Is Destroying Our Teenage Population and a Plan to Begin Solving the Problem. She suggests that because violence is a public health problem, we ought to be able to find ways to *prevent* violence in our society. First we have to examine and try to understand the many faces of violence.

HATE CRIMES

Racial hatred and bigotry cause many instances of violence. Nearly everyone knows the Rodney King story. Rodney King was a black man beaten by white police officers in Los Angeles. In the first trial, a jury acquitted the police. The riots that followed left fifty-eight people dead and property damage of more than one billion dollars. "To many blacks, the fact that the not-guilty verdicts were handed down by a jury that included no blacks . . . virtually proves that the criminal justice system is ruled by bias and that they cannot look to it for fair treatment," according to *Time* (May 11, 1992). The conviction of the two white policemen in the civil rights trial held later renewed the faith of some people in the criminal justice system.

In the *Los Angeles Times* (May 26, 1993) it was reported that a twenty-one-year-old sailor, Terry Helvey, faced a maximum sentence of life imprisonment for beating to death another twenty-one-year-old sailor, Allen Schindler, because Schindler was gay. The day after the murder, Helvey said he hated homosexuals and would do the same thing again. A psychiatrist testified that Helvey had suffered from child abuse, came from a broken home, and had been drinking heavily before the incident. He had also used muscle-building steroids, which may increase aggressive behavior.

More than a dozen states have enacted laws permitting courts to increase jail time for offenders who perpetrate crimes based on race, religion, ethnicity, gender, or sexual orientation. Such was the situation of Bradley Mills, sentenced to fifty years (more than double the twenty-two years suggested) for the murder of a Vietnamese-American student. The judge increased the sentence because the motivation for the crime was ethnicity.

In the example below, a derogatory label for a Mexican-American man set up a violent assault situation.

Caitlin, fifteen

"When my brother was about thirteen years old, he went to an Iron Maiden concert. After the concert, my mom and stepdad were waiting for him in a parking lot beside a fence. Little did they know—on the other side of the fence was trouble. A Latino man stole a souvenir shirt from one of my brother's friends. She yelled, "Stop it, Beaner!" Before my brother and his friends knew what was happening, they were surrounded. Another of my brother's friends got beaten up. Someone held a knife to my brother's throat. They told him to give up his leather jacket, which he did. He lost his contact lenses because they were in the pocket of his jacket. He also lost a souvenir shirt, but he felt lucky to be alive."

DRUG/GANG VIOLENCE

For those who have what they need, drug and gang violence is difficult to understand. But for those who have little in the way of stability, parental attention, or money, membership in such groups sometimes seems to be the only choice. In the world of these young people, nothing makes sense. Gang violence and the drug culture are the *result* of violence and in turn *cause* violence.

Below, two young men give their opinions about what's wrong in their environments.

Marvin, seventeen

"Many friends have died. Many friends have been shot, beaten, and hurt, but you are unlikely to be familiar with the circumstances of a young black male. I feel sad, but at the same time I am smacked up against reality."

Harold, eighteen

"Crime? There are too many stories, just too many. What do you mean, my 'reaction'? There's no reaction. It's life. It happens every day in my neighborhood. The worst part? Well, maybe an arrest or two. Some blood here and there? Does any good come out of it? Well, if it's stealing, and you get away with it, maybe that's good. But what goes around comes around. Right? I usually give fake names even for questioning. I don't want to take the blame for a crime done by somebody else. I like to keep to myself. What's not helpful? Police and their attitudes, peer pressure. If I were to give any advice, it would be this: Be aware. Crime is everywhere."

Léon Bing, author of *Do or Die*, spent four years with gangs in South Central Los Angeles, trying to understand "why." She says, "They're killing each other, and it's getting worse all the time. Their lives are so desolate, they have so little hope, and they are taking it out on people like themselves. Their parents, some of them, are on crack or other drugs. They have nothing you would recognize as family life, too little food, no future. Many of them are abused children. Nobody cares about them." Bing says these gang members have nothing to live for. They pledge allegiance to their neighborhood gang—and it becomes their whole world.

Others say that *alienation* is the key word. Kids join gangs to have a sense of belonging, to feel they are "somebody." Joining a gang makes them feel they've accomplished something even if what they've accomplished is negative and destructive.

Fortunately, not all gang members stay in gangs forever. Many of those who get out speak eloquently about their struggles. Three young Hispanic men, Moses, eighteen; Marcus, nineteen; and Cisco, twenty-one, are former gang members. As members of GRASP (Gang Rescue and Support Project), they give presentations to people of all ages.

Marcus was a cofounder of GRASP, a support group for those who want to leave gangs behind. He helped start the organization a couple of years ago after the gang-related death of his foster brother. Marcus, who at fifteen was living on the streets, said he didn't have anyone to talk to about his pain. He began trying to leave the gang because he was tired of seeing friends and relatives die.

For Moses, drugs and alcohol are a way of hiding from painful feelings. And yet he acknowledges that drinking has gotten him into a lot of trouble. He has already been shot three times—in the head, the back, and the leg. Moses says, "I'm eighteen, and I'm an alcoholic." He has cirrhosis of the liver; the doctor tells him if he doesn't stop drinking, he'll die young. But Moses doesn't want to die. He has a two-year-old child, and he wants to be a good role model for his son.

Cisco, who was in a gang for five years, has lost five friends to violent death. For selling cocaine, Cisco did two years in community corrections. Now, however, he has graduated from high school and is attending college. He says that at seventeen, he was a bully. When he pulled a gun on a kid, he thought he was getting respect. "But I wasn't getting respect," says Cisco. "I was using intimidation, and I was getting fear. For me, getting out of gangs depended on redefining the word 'respect.'" Attending an alternative high school helped him learn to respect his culture and his history. He has a new respect for his neighborhood too. "They call my neighborhood a ghetto," says Cisco, "but I call it home." Finally, he says, "Killing brown on brown is wrong. Killing black on black is wrong. Killing *anyone* is wrong."

In the past, these three young men felt as if they had no control of their destiny, but each found the strength to take control. Like the *participants* in gang violence, *victims* of gang violence often feel as if they have lost control.

Tyler, sixteen

"When I was six, I was standing at a corner by the crosswalk. I happened to be wearing red, a gang color. An older kid crossed in front of me and punched me in the stomach. I was scared because I had no idea what was happening. Just as the rest of the gang was coming at me, a car drove by, and the woman driver threatened to call the police. The police didn't help much. We filed a report, but nothing ever came of it. My parents tried to help me

understand why this person was beating on me. My advice to others is to learn whatever you can from it. Basically what I learned is that you don't have much control over what goes on in the world."

J.T., fifteen

"A friend of the family was the victim of a drive-by shooting in a dark alley. The friend knew the kids from school, and they were harassing him. He told them to leave him alone, and they shot him. His younger brother was with him when he died. The family didn't have enough money to pay for the hospital bills or for the funeral."

The father of a six-year-old critically wounded in cross-fire between rival gang members says that rather than teaching his son the ABCs, he wishes he had taught him to duck when he heard a loud noise.

Most authorities and ordinary citizens are so frustrated by gang activity that they don't know what to do next. Here are a few things you can do to combat gang violence:

- Keep outside lights on at night.
- If you hear gunshots or see a crime being committed, call 911 or other police numbers to report the location.
- Write or call your elected officials and tell them you expect them to pass new laws and enforce existing laws aimed at combatting drug and gang violence.
- Look for ways to help increase the dialogue among all members of your school and community.

FAMILIES IN TROUBLE

Another theory for the increase in crime by young people is that the parents who raise disturbed children are often in trouble themselves. They may be under the influence of drugs or alcohol, living in poverty, or too involved in their divorce, their social life, or their career. They may be very young and have inadequate parenting skills. Some experts say that children who have been abused and neglected or who have witnessed violence will in turn perpetrate violence. Other studies show that 70 percent of young offenders come from single-parent homes.

At the very least, a person who grows up in a home in which family violence and neglect are the norm will acquire little knowledge of nurturing behavior. The young person may be too wrapped up in her own problems to be able to care about the pain of others. Heather still feels bitter about her mother's indifference.

Heather, fourteen

"When I was about nine years old, my parents got a divorce. My mother got custody of me and my brother, who was five at the time. For me, the neglect lasted about three years. Many nights my mother left me alone to take care of my brother. She didn't come home until 3 or 4 a.m. Sometimes she brought men to spend the night. She didn't take us to the dentist for three years, and she never took us to the doctor— even when we were sick. She didn't care. She rarely bought us clothes, and when she did, she found the cheapest stuff available. Meanwhile she bought herself $500 outfits. She had (or has) a drinking/drug problem. I used to think she cared about me, but I

found out she doesn't. Two years ago, I moved in with my dad and stepmom."

Authorities believe this kind of "home alone" neglect is more common than most people realize. A child treated the way Heather's mother treated her does not grow up with a well-loved feeling.

In a highly publicized case, Sharon and David Schoo of St. Charles, Illinois, left their daughters, ages four and nine, alone while they went on vacation. According to an Associated Press story, the couple allegedly abused the children as well. The parents were accused of locking one daughter in a crawl space for several hours. They were said to have kicked one child in the ribs and abdomen and beaten both children with a belt.

Not long ago someone phoned 911 in the area of Fort Worth, Texas. The dispatcher who answered the call heard a woman's voice say, "I'm afraid my husband and I are bad parents. We haven't been feeding our child." Police traced the call and found a comatose thirteen-year-old boy chained to a kitchen cabinet. Steven Hill, who weighed only fifty-five pounds, never regained consciousness. The parents had resorted to withholding food when "the hitting wasn't working any longer."

In the example below, a young woman recalls physical abuse by her father.

Julie, fourteen

"When I was small, my father abused me. He slapped, hit, punched, pushed, and kicked me. I remember screaming because it hurt. But if I screamed or cried more, he hit me more. The reason he hit me was because he was an alcoholic. He's in jail now."

In 1991, according to the National Center for the Prevention of Child Abuse, parents physically, mentally, and sexually abused an estimated 2.7 million young people. Some teens subjected to this kind of violence become violent toward others—sometimes even to their abusive parents. Jacob, a fifteen-year-old arrested for murder in Colorado Springs, Colorado, told his teacher that he and a friend had killed Jacob's parents. "They hit me, and I couldn't take it any longer."

In the *New York Times* (July 26, 1993), it was reported that eighth-grade and fifth-grade brothers shot their father with a deer rifle. The boys told neighbors they were tired of his beatings and tired of watching him sexually molest their ten-year-old sister. Family counselors and the school principal faulted the system for failing to provide a way for the children to free themselves from the abuse. According the principal, the boys were "scared silent" by their father.

ENTERTAINMENT VIOLENCE

Many people believe that violence in the media is at least partly responsible for the increase in violent crimes by young people. Entertainment violence takes many forms. It includes representations of violence in children's toys and in video games, and actual acts of violence in movies and television. According to the American Psychological Association, a typical child sees 8,000 murders and 100,000 violent acts on TV before leaving elementary school.

In Milwaukee four teenage boys were implicated in the killing of a man who was driving home from a business meeting. The young men said they "got ideas" about winning power and respect through violence from two movies. According to the Scripps Howard News Service (June 3, 1993), the teenagers had seen one of the movies, "Menace II Society," hours before the killing. The movie is "a violent, bleak portrayal of young black males in south-central Los Angeles." One of the boys, fifteen, said that on the bus ride home they "were all hyped up from the action in the movie" and made a plan to rob someone at gunpoint. One of the boys had brought a .25-caliber handgun.

Constant exposure to violence "desensitizes" people. First finding media violence horrifying, they come to accept such behavior as "normal." According to the *Los Angeles Times* (March 24, 1993), Americans under age thirty are more likely than older Americans to watch violence on TV. Seventy-eight percent of Americans believe that "television shows so much violence that people grow up not being shocked by violence."

In a study begun in 1973, behaviorists at the University of British Columbia observed a small town as it received its first television signals. After two years of TV exposure, the children in the town became more verbally and physically aggressive.

Not long ago, the Associated Press reported that two ten-year-old boys in Liverpool, England, were being questioned in connection with the brutal slaying of a two-year-old boy who had wandered away from his mother at a shopping center. The killing sparked a national outcry in Great Britain. People called for a crackdown on the television violence they considered at least partially responsible for the killing.

A recent poll revealed that 79 percent of viewers thought that television programs either "strongly contribute" or "somewhat contribute" to societal violence. In addition, 86 percent believed that TV violence "strongly contributes" or "somewhat contributes" to violence among young people under eighteen.

Dennis Kennedy of Project PAVE believes that one of the problems with violence shown in movies and on television is its unreality. "Arnold Schwarzenegger shoots everyone in the room, and the camera follows him out the door." The camera fails to show the pain and agony of those left in the room to die or the grief of the survivors.

Males

Because the large majority of teenage offenders are male, some people blame that aggression on the male sex hormone. Others find this theory ridiculous. They believe a more plausible explanation is the societal conditioning of males to be "macho." Nevertheless, some experts blame crime on hereditary characteristics. In the book *Crime and Human Nature*, the authors, James Q. Wilson and Richard J. Herrnstein, present some characteristics of criminals:

- Young males are more likely to commit crimes than older males.
- Children from large families are more likely to become delinquent than children from smaller families.
- First-born boys commit *fewer* crimes than those born later in the birth order.
- Young men with a strong attachment to their mother are less likely to commit crimes than those with a weaker attachment to the mother.
- Criminals on the average are *less* intelligent than noncriminals.

- People who break the law often have "unusual" personalities.

In this chapter we've discussed some of the possible reasons violent crime is such a problem in today's society. The next chapter examines specific crimes and how to become a survivor.

CHAPTER ◇ 3

Violent Crimes

*H*omicide/manslaughter/murder: These words are
similar enough in meaning to be used inter-
changeably by the general public. The victim of
any of the three has been killed. Unfortunately, homicide,
manslaughter, and murder, especially by young people,
are becoming more common in our violent society.

Homicide is the killing of one person by another.
Manslaughter is the unlawful killing of another person
without previous intent to do so. *Murder* is premeditated
killing.

In the United States in 1991, nearly 25,000 murders
were committed. Bullets now cause one of every four
deaths of American teens. Arguments that used to be
"settled" with fists are now often settled permanently in
an instant. One person is dead, and another spends his
life behind bars. Often young people who have fired a
fatal shot would give anything to be able to go back to the
five minutes before the argument. Unfortunately, it's too
late.

Tony, fifteen

"For protection, one of my friends brought a gun to a party. There was a lot of alcohol involved. Everyone was drunk. There was an argument, and things got bad. The guy who was hosting the party told my friend to leave. My friend reached for his gun, but the other guy pulled his gun first and shot my friend in the chest. My friend died instantly. I think about him a lot and about his short life. It hurts to know he's gone. The advice I give to people my age is, 'Live a smart life, stay out of trouble, and keep away from guns.'"

Nearly 4,200 teenagers died from gunshots in 1990, up from 2,500 in 1985. Every 22 minutes an American is shot, stabbed, beaten, or strangled to death. More people than ever before are being killed by strangers, and an increasing number of murders are going unsolved.

Sarah, seventeen

"Very close friends of our family were murdered. They were like relatives, so we called the parents 'aunt' and 'uncle.' A man entered their house through the attached garage. He probably only planned to rob them. But the father got up to check on things. The burglar killed him and then proceeded to kill the mother and the oldest daughter. He tried to kill the younger daughter too, but she escaped and is the only one still alive. She lives with her grandparents.

"The worst part is that such good people were taken away for no reason, and that the person who

*did it was never found. My family helped me deal
with the grief and pain. My advice to anyone who
has to go through something like this is to rely on
family and friends who will give you support. You're
hurting. Mourn. It's okay; you have to do it."*

Homicide, manslaughter, and murder all leave terrible
pain that never entirely goes away.

Joe, seventeen

*"One night my mother was strangled at a nightclub.
She had left the club to go get something out of her
purse. She never came back. I really don't know
much about what happened because I was only six
years old. I do know that I was sad and mad at the
same time. To this day I want revenge—if only I
could find out who did it. I always feel sad when
another person mentions his mother. It hurts deep
down inside. My grandmother raised me and my
older brother and sister. As I was growing up, people
always asked me, 'What happened to your mother?'
Of course, I didn't have a mother anymore."*

SEXUAL ASSAULT

Ranking close to homicide in its devastation and violation
of the victim is sexual assault, which includes rape and
related crimes. Rape victims often have higher levels of
stress than victims of other crimes. Sexual assault victims
may feel like Humpty Dumpty, broken into a million
pieces. Some rape victims can barely talk about what happened. In discussing the rape of her friend, Emily's words
explode like gunshots: "Gang rape. Band of foreigners.

California. At a gas station in the open. Couldn't believe she could keep a secret that big for so long."

Rape is a crime of violence motivated by the desire to control and dominate. Although the exact definition of rape varies from state to state, forced sexual acts are usually considered rape. *Acquaintance rape* is forced sexual intercourse or other sexual acts occurring between people who know each other. *Date rape* is forced sexual intercourse or other sexual acts that occur in a dating situation.

In the book *Recovery*, Helen Benedict presents five myths about rape.

Myth #1: Rape is sex.

Fact: Rape is an act of violence in which sex is used as a weapon.

Myth #2: Rape is motivated by lust.

Fact: The word "lust" implies frustrated sexual desire or passion, but sexual passion has little to do with rape. The rapist is motivated by anger, the desire to control, the urge to make another person suffer, or a combination of all three.

Myth #3: The rapist is a weird loner.

Fact: Rapists may appear as normal as anyone. The difference is that they fail to see their victims as human beings with the right to say no.

Myth #4: Women provoke rape.

Fact: That statement is ridiculous. It causes

other people to blame the victim and often causes the victim to blame herself.

Myth #5: Only bad women get raped.

Fact: Rape is a crime against people—of all ages, of all economic classes, and of all races and ethnic groups. Males can also be rape victims.

More than twelve million American women have been raped at least once in their lives, according to *Time* (May 4, 1992). Even more surprising, 61 percent of the victims were younger than eighteen at the time of the rape. The largest number (32.3 percent) were between the ages of eleven and seventeen. The second largest number (29.3 percent) were younger than eleven. Twenty-two percent were between eighteen and twenty-four. In almost 80 percent of the cases, the victim knew the rapist.

National studies have shown that alcohol and drugs are involved in up to 70 percent of acquaintance and date rapes among high school and college students. Sometimes it is the rapist who has been drinking; sometimes it is the victim.

Allison, seventeen

"I was at a party at my boyfriend's house. He was drinking and doing drugs. He asked me to go to his room with him. He wanted to show me his new drum set. When we got there, he locked the door. I guess you could say the rest is history. A few months later, he moved. Two days before Christmas, he killed himself.

"Right after the rape, I was scared. Later, I felt

cheap and used. After he killed himself, I blamed myself for his suicide. I had nightmares and felt that I couldn't trust any of my male friends. I was too scared to tell anyone. I turned to drinking and drugs and pretended I didn't care. My advice to anyone else who has to deal with rape is, 'Tell someone immediately.'"

The Ultimate Violation

The crime of rape and other sexual assaults create the same feeling of violation that victims of other crimes endure. Rape victims, however, experience the ultimate violation. The victim not only loses control but suffers intrusion into her innermost being. Rape is not a sexual act. The rapist *uses* a sexual act to humiliate the victim.

More women are coming forward to report rapes, but many women are only too ready to blame themselves. Other young women say they would report the rape if they could count on their name not being used. According to current estimates, only about 16 percent of rape victims report the assault to the police, but this low percentage may be rising.

Although males constitute about 10 percent of rape victims, they are less likely to report the crime because of the stigma connected with rape. Our society's stereotype of males is that they are macho, dominant, and in control at all times. For any male to admit that he is a survivor of rape puts him in an inferior, victimized position. Many males prefer to suffer in silence. Silence, however, is unhealthy for the survivor.

Cory, eighteen

"Last summer I was working as a milk deliveryman. I started my route in the dark. One morning when I got back into my truck, two young guys with guns were waiting for me. They were both drunk, and they demanded money. I said I didn't have any. I'd heard about males getting raped in prison. Well, guess what? Until now I never told anyone."

SEXUAL HARASSMENT

Another form of violence most often directed at women is sexual harassment. One definition of sexual harassment is "mind rape," but it can be much more than that. Some experts divide sexual harassment into categories. *Visual* sexual harassment includes staring and sexual gestures. The *verbal* type includes wolf whistles, sexual jokes, and threatening sexual comments. *Physical* forms of sexual harassment include touching, pinching, grabbing, rubbing, or unwanted closeness.

Author Liz Kelly says that sexual harassment exists on a continuum from less violent to more violent. Repeated invitations to date despite rejections, sexual propositions, attempted rape, and rape itself are all forms of sexual harassment and/or assault. According to Kelly, the point at which sexual harassment crosses the line into sexual assault is unclear.

If two people are equally interested in a relationship and participate equally, that is not sexual harassment. Like rape, sexual harassment is coercive and has little to do with sex. Instead, it is a power play.

Tiffany, eighteen

"I was a waitress at the time, and I had a manager who always made sexually suggestive comments. He brushed my rear with his hand, he made inquiries about the private lives of my boyfriend and me, he gave me the worst schedule and the worst sections. My immediate reaction was to keep quiet until I figured out what was going on. Eventually I couldn't keep quiet any longer. I felt forced to quit. Now I'm broke while looking for another job.

"I believe any victim of sexual harassment should confront the person and his supervisor. I should have said, 'You are sexually harassing me, and you need to stop now.' That would have told him that I recognized what he was doing, and it would have embarrassed him in front of everyone else in the restaurant."

Women are beginning to strike back. When Anita Hill alleged that her former boss, Supreme Court nominee Clarence Thomas, had sexually harassed her, many people did not believe her story. But Hill gave women the courage to come forward with other accounts of sexual harassment. Younger women are also subject to sexual harassment by male bosses.

Although adult males are more often guilty of sexual harassment than females, sometimes the *victim* is male. In the *Los Angeles Times* (May 20, 1993), it was reported that a jury awarded a million dollars in damages to a man. The jury found that a woman, the chief financial officer of a spa manufacturer, sexually harassed Sabin Gutierez of Ontario, California. An attorney involved in the case said the verdict was probably the first in the country in favor of a man suing a woman for sexual harassment.

Sexual harassment can take place in the street, at school, or at work.

Elizabeth, seventeen

"I was working as a lifeguard. The head guard called women sexual names and graphically described sexual acts. One day I'd had enough, and I told him to stop using those terms because they offended me. I said if he continued, I would inform his supervisor. My friend also told him that his talk offended her. He finally stopped, but some people said I should have told his supervisor anyway."

Sexual harassment at work is outlawed by the 1991 Civil Rights Act, which provides up to $300,000 in damage awards to victims. However, only a few states have looked carefully at sexual harassment of young people in school situations. *Newsweek* (October 19, 1992) quoted Pat Callbeck Harper, a gender-equality specialist for the Montana schools: "There are things that go on in the hallways, the parking lots, at band practice, that are as bad if not worse" (than sexual harassment in the workplace).

A recent national study by the Association of University Women found that 81 percent of students (85 percent of girls and 76 percent of boys) reported having been sexually harassed at school. On the other hand, two thirds of the boys and half of the girls admitted that *they* had harassed *others* at school. The survey covered fourteen categories of harassment, including sexual comments, jokes, and gestures; touching, grabbing, or pinching in a sexual way; spreading sexual rumors; spying on someone showering or dressing; name-calling, using such words as slut, whore, dog, or fag; making catcalls and whistles; passing unwanted sexual pictures or notes; forcing someone against his or her will to kiss someone else; and blocking or cornering another person in a sexual way.

Brooke, sixteen

Brooke is thoughtful of others and their feelings. Although she has never encouraged the overly friendly gestures of Todd, a long-time acquaintance, she is always polite to him. Recently in a coed body-building class, the group did a series of push-ups. When the teacher's back was turned, Todd jumped on top of Brooke. She screamed. The teacher turned around and rolled her eyes at Brooke, who decided to keep quiet and not make a scene. When the class went to the wall to do knee-strengthening exercises, Brooke joined the rest. While another student distracted the teacher, Todd slipped his hand up Brooke's shorts. She screamed again. Todd shrugged. "I don't get it," he said aloud. "Something's wrong with Brooke today."

What should Brooke have done? First, she should have confronted Todd directly. If she wanted to avoid a scene, she could have spoken to him after class or called him at home. If Todd didn't stop the harassment (or even if he did), Brooke could have talked to the physical education teacher. Another good idea might have been to get a group of girls together to see if *they'd* had trouble with Todd. The next step could have been a Letter-to-the-Editor of the school paper. A united group protesting sexual harassment and giving specific examples carries a great deal of clout. The group could also take their concerns to the principal. Finally, students or their parents can file a complaint with the federal government within 180 days of an alleged offense. The federal courthouse nearest you can help you find the address of your regional office of the U.S. Department of Education, Office of Civil Rights.

Some authorities define sexual harassment in schools as any sexual incident that makes a student feel unsafe and insecure. Especially dangerous are adults such as teachers and coaches who sexually harass students from a position of power or authority.

Lauren, fifteen

"I was sexually harassed at school. One of the coaches was more interested in me than he should have been. He stared at me wherever I went. He tried to get me alone. He touched me (usually on my back). He started changing clothes in front of me. He made it a point to stand close to me; he made sexual comments. He followed me. He sat by me on bus trips. He showed up in some of my classes. His presence around me all the time kept guys my age away. I didn't want to be around him. I didn't talk to him. I was scared.

"Now I always look behind me to see if he's there. I don't feel safe in many places. I find myself wondering exactly what people mean in their words and looks. I have lost a lot of trust in people."

Lauren's panic is similar to that experienced by many victims of posttraumatic stress disorder (PTSD), which is discussed further in Chapter 4.

ASSAULT, MUGGING, AND ROBBERY

Assault, mugging, and robbery all involve either the *threat* of physical harm or *actual* physical harm. A robbery may turn out to be less intrusive than an assault, but the victim is still threatened. Victims may feel shame because they have not been able to defend themselves. They have lost control. In addition, some victims have to deal with the loss of valuable possessions.

Exactly what are these crimes? Let's start with *assault*, an intentional physical attack by one human being against another. In a worst-case scenario, a person tries to inflict bodily harm on another and may even use a deadly weapon.

Amanda, eighteen

Amanda's parents made sure she didn't work at a restaurant that stayed open late at night. The Wooden Spoon, which closed at 9 p.m., was a family place. Amanda's parents didn't know that several nights a week Amanda and only one other person "closed" the restaurant.

One night at about 9:30, Amanda went into the storeroom to turn off the outside lights. She was so familiar with the location of the switches that she didn't bother to turn on the storeroom lights. Suddenly someone hit her on the head with a ketchup bottle. She fell to the floor unconscious while her assailant ran out the back door. No one ever figured out the motive for the assault, and the attacker was never found.

Amanda's parents demanded that she quit her job, but Amanda put on a brave face to her parents and to the world. "It's a good thing it wasn't a jar of mustard," she said. "That might have given me a worse headache." Inside, Amanda was hurting.

Amanda's secure work world had been shattered. She had nightmares, panic attacks, and migraine headaches for months afterward. She didn't want to go back to work, but she needed the money. Also, she refused to admit to her parents that they had been right and she had been wrong.

Not all assaults are by strangers. Domestic violence, sometimes called *battered woman's syndrome*, is any kind of assault by a partner, married or otherwise.

Jessica, fifteen

"My dad was abusive, verbally and physically, to my mom. One day he got angry about something and beat her so badly that she was in the hospital for a week. I was only a baby and don't remember it. When I got older, Mom told me about it. Luckily for us, she was smart enough to get out of the relationship. She became a physician and now speaks out about domestic violence. She's very involved in the Domestic Violence Coalition. My dad went to jail where he belonged."

According to the FBI, domestic violence is the least reported crime in America. People usually don't talk about it; they are embarrassed, afraid, or fail to realize what is happening to them. And yet, assaults at home are the main cause of injury for women between the ages of fifteen and forty-four. More than half of all female murder victims have been killed by boyfriends, former boyfriends, husbands, or ex-husbands.

It is estimated that a woman is battered every eighteen seconds. When most people think of domestic violence, they think of husbands hurting their wives. But domestic violence by boyfriends injures 25 percent of young unmarried women. Some authorities estimate that physical abuse occurs in about 60 percent of all intimate relationships. Even more scary: About half of all males questioned think this kind of assault is okay.

Andrea, twenty

"I'd been living with my boyfriend for a year when it first happened. He slapped me. Afterward he felt real bad about it. He kept saying he was sorry, and the next day he sent me a dozen long-stemmed roses. Then about six months later, it happened again. This time we both tried to figure out why. His car had broken down, and he had no way to get to work. He was under a lot of stress. He said he was sorry he'd taken out his frustration on me. He even cried and begged me to forgive him. He hugged and kissed me and said things would be okay."

Unfortunately for Andrea, the incidents of violence got more severe and more frequent. No matter what the excuse or the apology, no one has the right to abuse someone else. Andrea didn't realize until much later that she and her boyfriend were caught up in a cycle of violence.

The Cycle of Violence

The cycle of violence in a relationship has three stages that go round and round like the hands of a clock.

Stage One: For whatever reason, anger and tension build. The abusive boyfriend or husband feels an increasing need to try to control his partner.

Stage Two: The batterer "snaps" and delivers a punch, a slap, a kick, or a push to the victim. Or the battering may go on for several minutes or even hours.

Stage Three: The batterer feels bad about what he has done and expresses regret. He may blame the victim, he may promise never to do such a thing again, and he may give gifts of affection and material things. The victim forgives, and the cycle is ready to begin again.

Facts to Remember

- Even if the offender tries to blame you, the battering is not your fault. You are not responsible for making him angry, any more than you will be able to make him return to the loving person he was when you met him.
- Battering is rarely a one-time incident. The frequency and severity usually increase with time.
- Battering is against the law.
- Many victims remain in an abusive relationship because of fear, lack of money or support, lack of

belief in themselves, or the belief that the abuse will stop if they wait long enough.

• The victim cannot stop the violence. The only thing that works is the criminal-justice system with its consequences and treatment for the offender. To be effective, the treatment and the educational process often take from one to five years.

• The victim is in the greatest danger when trying to leave the relationship, but it is still better to leave than to stay.

Leaving an abusive relationship can lead to stalking.

Stalking

Stalking is a relatively new word when used in relation to people. It used to mean the way hunting animals sought out their prey. Today those who "stalk" are often abusers. Stalking means "to pursue or follow in a stealthy, furtive, or persistent manner."

According to some estimates, 200,000 people in the United States are stalking another person. Those being stalked or mercilessly harassed are lovers and coworkers, celebrities and ordinary citizens. Most are women.

In 1990 California passed the first state law making stalking a felony; since that time, a majority of states have passed similar laws. In 1993, Senator Bob Krueger of Texas, whose family had been victimized by a stalker, and Senator Barbara Boxer of California introduced a bill in Congress to make stalking a federal offense. Punishment— whenever a stalker crossed state lines or used the mail or telephone to make a threat—would be up to ten years in prison.

Often, short of moving to another country, there seems

little one can do to escape a stalker. But technological advances may eventually make it possible to track them.

Mugging

Mugging is an assault with robbery as the main motive.

Adam, fifteen

"I got mugged for my shoes. I was shocked. The worst part was that I wasn't able to get away. The second worst part was having people watch like it was a show or something. They didn't help at all. But at least I gained some understanding: Now I know how it feels to have something I value taken away by someone who has no right to it."

Brad, fifteen

"I was walking home from school with my friend when this guy asked us if we had any money. We said no, which was true. I really didn't have any money. So he punched me in the stomach and ran off."

Robbery

Robbery is the actual taking of property in the immediate possession of another person. In this way it is distinguished from burglary, which is taking something from a house or business. In robbery, force or the threat of force may be involved. The robber may also use a weapon.

Lance, eighteen

"My brother, who graduated from high school two years ago, was robbed by two guys. He only had

three bucks. After they took his money, they punched him in the mouth and chipped his tooth. We called the cops and got the guys arrested. We sued them and made them pay to fix my brother's tooth."

In some parts of the country, young people are being assaulted, mugged, or robbed for athletic clothes with team logos—a professional team sports jacket, for example. Some of these robbers are gang members; others simply enjoy "jacking" another person. The robbers aren't fussy about which team or logo they pick. The Dallas Cowboys, Chicago White Sox, Los Angeles Raiders, Miami Dolphins, New York Giants—you name it, someone takes it. If you do wear such a jacket or anything else another person demands, hand it over. It's better to lose a jacket than your life.

Pickpocketing and Bag-Snatching

Pickpocketing and bag-snatching are other crimes that can turn violent. Half a million people in the United States are victims of these crimes each year.

Claire, fifteen

"Once in Oklahoma City we needed a map because we were looking for a friend's house. We parked our van at a 7–11, and my dad went in. We'd been driving all day, and it was really hot, so we had the car doors and windows open. My brother was asleep, and my mom was in the back seat, reading. This huge dude came out of an alley and jumped into our van. He spotted my mom's purse and took off with it. Mom ran after him, but it was no use. He got $500, some credit cards, and our family's passports."

Locked car doors might have prevented this instance of purse-snatching. Claire and her family members were lucky; the criminal did not physically hurt them.

In the example below, a young woman witnesses violence to her mother, the victim of a purse-snatching.

Debbie, sixteen

"When I was eight years old, my mother and I were about to go into a supermarket when this woman attacked my mother. She was trying to get Mom's purse, but my mother put up a fight. When I realized what was happening, I ran into the store and asked a cashier to help. We found my mother lying on the sidewalk with this woman smashing Mom's head into the concrete. The police came and caught the woman. It turned out she was a drug dealer, and this was about her tenth offense. She got a long prison sentence. My mother isn't paralyzed, but she has a lot of pain in her neck."

Security expert Louis Mizell warns people to be aware of the imaginative tricks these criminals use. In one trick he calls the "ketchup squirt," a member of the pickpocketing team squirts ketchup on the victim's clothes. While another offers to help the victim clean up, a third team member grabs the victim's purse or wallet. Another trick is called the "people press," in which the pickpocket tries to confuse and distract you so that he can take your belongings. In the example below, a young man became an instant victim.

Jordan, fifteen

"I was in the mall the day after Christmas with three friends. We were minding our own business when four older men bumped into us. I didn't realize until a few minutes later that they had taken my wallet with $20 in it."

Beware of the Automatic Teller Machine (ATM)

Whether or not you want to believe it, automatic teller machines can be hazardous to your health. The machines themselves aren't dangerous, but the people who hang around them may be.

Doug, eighteen

"I had a date with a cute girl named Kelli. I wanted to impress her, so I borrowed my dad's car. Unfortunately, I forgot to take money, but I didn't realize my mistake until after I'd picked Kelli up. It was about 8:30 at night, and we were on our way to a movie. No problem, I thought, I'll just stop at my bank. I stopped right in front of the machine, which is on a pretty busy street. When I hopped out, I was talking to Kelli. I wasn't paying attention to anything else. As soon as I got the money (fifty bucks), this guy appears out of nowhere, snatches the money, and starts walking away.

"Like a fool, I went after him. I don't know what I said. Something like, 'Hey, that's my money.'

"Meanwhile Kelli jumps out of the car and says, 'Don't!' That was all she said. Later she explained she meant it for me, as in 'Don't go after him.' But he

might have thought she was talking to him, as in, 'Don't take the money.'

"Anyway he kept walking, but he threw a ten-dollar bill over his shoulder. I was shaking so much I could hardly pick it up. I got back in the car. Kelli and I just sat there for a minute holding hands. I guess we both realized how lucky we were."

If you must use an ATM, here are a few safety tips:

- Choose an ATM in a well-used, well-lighted area, free of obvious hiding places.
- Try to go during daylight hours and don't go to the same machine at the same time each day.
- Count your money away from the machine.
- Don't let anyone see your personal identification number, and never give it to anyone.
- Stay alert and do your business quickly.

Make a Plan

In the book *The Danger Zone*, Patricia Harmon suggests making a plan. The best way to be prepared for an assault or robbery is to go through possible scenarios in your mind. For example, imagine yourself driving back to school for an evening meeting. You've just gotten your license, and you're pleased with the trust your parents have placed in you.

You're a little late for the meeting and all the nearby spaces are taken, so you have to park a block away from school. You're making sure your car doors are locked when someone appears out of nowhere and puts a gun to your ribs. "This is a stick-up. Give me your wallet."

You are prepared to make no sudden moves that will

scare the robber. You may be shaking all over, but you give him the wallet. When you're sure he's gone, you run to the school and get help.

If the robber has your keys, get your locks changed as soon as possible. Later, if you notice anyone suspicious lurking around your house, call the police.

Going over all this in your mind before an incident will help you feel as prepared as anyone can in such a situation.

Other Crimes

In the past, most people considered burglary and bike and car theft nonviolent crimes. Usually the victim was not harmed, at least not physically. But even if you are not hurt in such an incident, you still feel violated. Victims report having the same feelings of loss and fear as the victims of more serious crimes.

Suzanne, fifteen

"Some people broke into the house through my window and trashed my room. They wrote obscene words on my mirror with lipstick. They didn't go through the rest of the house, either because they only wanted to scare me—which they did—or because the dogs were inside. The people who did it knew my name because they wrote, 'We'll be back, Suzanne!' I felt invaded and scared half to death."

Alex, fourteen

"While Dad was mowing the front lawn, someone went into the garage and stole all his power tools. They tried to break the lock on the door to the house.

When Dad went into the garage, his tools were gone, the door to the house was chopped up, and the car window was broken."

Home Security

You can never make your home or your belongings absolutely burglarproof, but you can do some things to increase your chances of safety.

- When you're inside, especially if you're alone, keep doors locked and windows closed. If you don't use them, all the locks in the world won't keep your things (and you) safe.
- When you go outside to play basketball or work in the yard, lock the door and take a key.
- Don't leave purses or other valuables right inside an open back or side door. Some thieves have very long fingers.
- If you have bikes and other important equipment in your garage, close the garage door when you leave the area.
- Always lock your bike, even in the garage.
- Use available resources. Buy or borrow a book from the library on how to increase the security of your home. A locksmith may be willing to give you a free assessment in the hope that you will hire the firm to upgrade your home security. Or ask your local police department for a walk-though.

In the United States, a car is stolen every nineteen seconds. That adds up to a grand total of 1.7 million vehicles a year. Most of them are stolen when the owner has parked the car and left.

Eric, eighteen

"My gauge read empty, so I stopped to get some gas. I left the car running and went inside to pay. When I came out, the car was gone. I thought it was some kind of joke—like my friend had taken it, but he hadn't. I had to ride the bus home and then listen to my parents tell me it was my fault."

Nowadays with more and more guns in circulation, riding in a car or riding a bike can turn dangerous. In 1991 armed carjackers stole approximately 28,000 cars. One way of increasing your personal safety is to keep your car doors locked at all times. Other ways to prevent car theft are discussed in Chapter 8. The next chapter looks at ways to help you make the transition from victim to survivor.

CHAPTER 4

Transition: Victim
to Survivor

Immediately after experiencing a violent crime, a person is a victim. The challenge facing every victim is to become a survivor. Exactly what each victim does to survive and even to triumph over the effects of the crime is up to that person. Chronic victims are people who let past events dictate their future; survivors are those who take action and work at overcoming the past.

No one can tell you exactly what to do to become a survivor, but a few principles may help. One is to be active, to do something. Neighbors who have been terrorized by thugs invading their homes become survivors by banding together in neighborhood watch groups.

Sexual abuse can be survived. Men who rape women are trying to control them. When women refuse to be quiet, but speak out against their attackers, they become survivors.

Molly, twenty

In Denver in 1992, a serial rapist was arrested and accused of raping at least a dozen women in one neighborhood. A number of women testified to having been raped at knifepoint or gunpoint in their homes. One of these witnesses was Molly, a Harvard University sophomore.

She agreed to be identified and photographed because she believes that speaking out helps. It shows others that rape doesn't have to ruin your life. Molly said that speaking out—to newspapers, friends, family, and to prospective colleges in her applications—helped the healing process. Although talking about the rape was painful, especially at first, this courageous young woman found that talking "brings more good than pain."

HEALING

Recovery and long-term survival cannot be rushed; healing may take a long time. Obviously, the victim of a homicide will not come back, but the victim's loved ones need help to go on living. Getting over the effects of other violent crimes may take a relatively short time, as in the case of bicycle theft, or years, as in most cases of rape.

If you are a victim of a violent crime, safety is the most important first step in the short term. If you come home from school and find the glass in your patio door broken, don't go inside to have a look around. Go next door and call the police or 911. If you are the victim of rape or assault of any kind, your first priority is getting safe. Call the police, your family, or a friend to take you to a hospital. Getting safe means getting help. If you are injured, you need immediate medical attention.

If you are a rape victim, do not eat, drink, wash, or change clothes until you have seen a doctor. Unpleasant as this may seem, the police need you "as is" to collect evidence.

Victims of violent crime have different needs, depending on the crime and its severity. A person victimized at home may need to get out of the house immediately. A person victimized away from home may want to get back to a familiar place as soon as possible. One person may need to cry; another may want to scream. You may need to be with other people; someone else may want to be alone. One rape victim may ask for help from a rape crisis center; another may seek the services of a private counselor. In any case, you may need to remind your friends and family that helping does not mean telling you it was all your fault, telling you to be quiet or to "calm down," or in general bossing you around.

After a violent crime, the victim's whole family may also suffer feelings of disorganization and disorientation. Most likely these feelings are the result of *stress*.

Stress

The noted expert on stress Dr. Hans Selye defined stress as "a reaction to any change in the environment." According to this definition, stress can be the result of *positive* or *negative* events. Even if stress is a reaction to positive events, it can become overwhelming. Wedding plans, for example: Have you ever participated in one of these "happenings"? In response to what should be a pleasant event, participants often become so "stressed out" that they start growling at each other.

In this chapter, we are referring to negative stresses, the kind that result from being the victim of a violent crime or, in some instances, many violent crimes.

Kim, fifteen

"A close friend was sexually molested, and another close friend was raped. Several friends have been victims of parental neglect. I've had a knife drawn on me twice, and a friend had a 12-gauge pulled on him. Many times I've had personal possessions taken at school. Also, someone stole my purse and dumped the contents in front of the cafeteria."

Ryan, seventeen

"Almost all my friends have had their bikes stolen. Our house has been burglarized. My car radio has been stolen twice. I was jumped while walking home at night. My sister was sexually harassed. I got into a major fight when a guy tried to take my coat."

Anxiety

Not only do crime victims suffer from stress, they also experience anxiety. One person describes anxiety this way: "It feels as if you have carbonated water in your blood vessels." Anxiety is a vague feeling that builds up in anticipation of a stressful event. Say, for example, that on Monday you come home to a sidewalk full of broken glass. Someone has smashed your kitchen window. Angry at being unable to get in, they pried open your back door with a crowbar. Anxiety is one of the feelings you have on Monday night and again on Tuesday after such violence.

When you come home on Tuesday, you feel anxious in anticipation of another chaotic scene.

Unsettling as it is, anxiety can help you by protecting you from danger. On Tuesday you will approach your house with caution.

But anxiety can also be destructive. If it builds up with no release, you may experience a state of chronic stress. Kerry talks about techniques she used to relieve her anxiety.

Kerry, sixteen

"I'm getting better every day. For a while after it happened, I felt anxiety and panic. But I learned that other people in similar circumstances often feel the same way. That was nice to know. And when I wanted to slit my wrists, I had a list of emergency numbers to call first. I used them, and that helped too. Sometimes for no reason my heart raced, and I found myself breathing hard, and I thought I was going to faint. Then I'd say, 'Kerry, get control,' and I'd go take a bubble bath. I'd stretch out in the tub and take long deep breaths. Then I'd play my relaxation tape. Now all I have to do is think *about my bubble bath or my tape and the anxiety passes."*

Ways of Coping with Stress

Most of us can get rid of reasonable amounts of stress by crying or laughing, by talking to family and friends, by exercising with regularity, by meditating, by doing something fun and relaxing, or by doing nothing at all. One easy stress reliever is deep breathing. Inhale while you count slowly to three, then count to three again as you exhale.

When deep breathing has made you feel relaxed, try *imaging.* First, tell yourself to de-stress. Then make images in your mind of a time when you were stress-free. Imagine a vacation at the beach or a ski trip in the mountains. Imagine these trips in as much detail as possible—colors, smells, tastes, textures, temperatures, and your emotions at the time.

Another way of dealing with negative feelings and stress is to write a letter to the person who victimized you—or you might want to write to the judge. Be as free with your language as you like. When you have finished, you may mail the letter—or you may decide to burn it and scatter the ashes in a significant place.

Adrienne, sixteen

Adrienne, a girl of strong religious faith, wrote the following letter to the people who had victimized various members of her family.

"Dear Criminals:

"I personally have not yet been a crime victim, but I worry that I will. My mom is blind, so a crime is especially terrifying to her. Our home has been burglarized three times in the twenty-five years we have lived here. During one of the break-ins, Mom was home by herself. If you were the burglar, thanks for not hurting my mom.

"My older sisters were victims of rape and attempted rape. A neighbor raped my oldest sister the day before my seventh birthday. I was too young to understand. Another sister was almost raped at work during a robbery. She was pregnant at the time.

If you were the rapist, I hope your conscience is bothering you, and I pray that God will help you.
                                    Love and God bless,
                                    Adrienne

"After I wrote that letter," says Adrienne, "I felt as if a huge weight had fallen off my shoulders. Of course, I never mailed the letter. Where would I have sent it?" At the time of the writing, however, it gave Adrienne a way of coping with stress.

Rather than escalating your stress by using sarcasm and put-downs, try eliminating them from your vocabulary. Instead, give sincere compliments to others and to yourself. Those around you will feel better, and you will too.

If all else fails, wrap a tennis racket in a towel, warn others in the household, and beat on your bed. Every time the bed takes a hit, shout out your feelings: "I am stressed. I am angry. I'm furious at the person who stole my bike." Or make up variations. You can get the same results by hitting tennis balls against the garage door, doing push-ups, or raking leaves.

POSTTRAUMATIC STRESS DISORDER

The term posttraumatic stress disorder (PTSD) describes the disorganization some people feel when they lose their sense of self-control. It is much more severe than the feelings caused by ordinary stress.

Violence causes a person to feel helpless, powerless, and overcome with fear. Stephanie, a victim of attempted rape, says, "I couldn't react, I couldn't move, I couldn't scream, I couldn't do anything." Courtney describes her feelings of helplessness when no one would come to her aid.

Courtney, seventeen

"When I was between seven and nine, my mom worked nights, so my aunt baby-sat for me. I used to go over there after school to spend the night. My uncle's brother was living with them at the time. Every night after the rest of the household had gone to sleep, he would come into my room and sexually molest me. It wasn't until I was twelve that I got up the courage to say something.

"At that point, I was crying out for someone to help me. We went to court, but no one believed me. I felt like the criminal. It seemed as if people didn't want to be around me. I felt scared and alone. Luckily, Mom believed me. She was the only one, but I guess one person is all you need."

Categories of PTSD

Judith Herman, author of *Trauma and Recovery*, divides the symptoms of posttraumatic stress disorder into three categories. The first is *hyperarousal*. The person has trouble sleeping, startles easily, and feels irritable. Hyperarousal often includes the feeling that the danger could reappear at any moment.

In Chapter 3, Sarah told of her reactions to the murders of three close family friends. She also experienced hyperarousal. "I was completely terrified. I believed that the person who killed three people in one family would somehow find me and try to kill me. I still feel jumpy at night. (It happened six years ago.) I always check all the doors before I go to bed. I think of my friend often and re-member how she looked in her coffin, and I feel afraid."

The second category, *intrusion*, means reliving the event as if it were occurring in the present. Another victim of attempted rape, Christina, fifteen, says the events replay in her mind like a movie scene that won't quit. "I went to a party with a friend. She left with someone she met there, and I was stuck. I had to find a way home. This one guy seemed okay, so I asked him to give me a ride. He had two friends with him, and they were both drunk. When we all got into the car, the three of them started saying mean things about girls and women. They started touching me and then tried to rip off my clothes. I ended up with bruises on the insides of my thighs. The whole night keeps playing over and over in my mind."

Numbing is the third category; the victim or witness in some way alters his or her state of consciousness to block out memories of the event. Victims describe this process as hypnotizing themselves, going into a trance-like state, forgetting the whole experience, or watching events unfold from somewhere outside their own bodies.

Anne, sixteen

"When I was fourteen, I met this guy named Paul. When we had known each other for about four months, he asked me to go to his house and help him do the dishes. So I went over there, and we did the dishes. When we were done, I sat on the futon to watch TV. He sat down beside me and started touch-ing me and finally used his weight to hold me down. Then he raped me. I went to a friend's house to take a shower. After I got out of the shower, I fainted.

Now whenever I look back on that experience, it's as if I'm sitting on that futon watching what happened to me happen to someone on the TV."

If victims understand the possibility of any or all of the above reactions, they will be better prepared if they occur. A violent crime such as the rape Anne describes can be devastating to anyone. But for a young person just beginning to be independent, it may feel even worse. The crime can make her vulnerable to feelings of guilt or of not measuring up to some ideal. Dr. Herman observes, "No matter how brave and resourceful the victim may have been, her actions were insufficient to ward off disaster."

Anne tells what happened after the rape. "When I regained consciousness, my friend let me lie down in her room. Meanwhile Paul came knocking at her front door. She didn't let him in. Then my mom came and took me to the hospital. A year later, I tried to kill myself and spent a year in a mental hospital."

Dr. Herman adds that after a rape it is common for the victim instead of the perpetrator to feel guilty. "Guilt may be understood as an attempt to draw some useful lesson from disaster and to regain some sense of power and control. To imagine that one could have done better may be more tolerable than to face the reality of utter helplessness." Sometimes people feel guilty because they are angry about what happened but they believe anger is not an acceptable emotion.

Remembering

Remembering and telling the story of what happened sometimes helps. Because victims of violent crime experience loss of power, they have to integrate what happened to them into their life story. This step is necessary to re-empower the victims and reconnect them with people and with life.

Survivors of crime rarely find much good in their experience, but some mention a greater determination to take care of themselves and to look after others. In the Prologue to *Beyond Survival*, crime victim Theresa Saldana says she wrote the book "to show how essential it is to create something positive out of an ugly, wrenchingly painful experience."

As a result of their experiences, many victims become strong survivors. But don't expect to bounce back immediately and be just as you were before the crime. You may never be exactly the same again. Becoming a stronger person and finding good in a bad experience are not like finding the pot of gold at the end of the rainbow. A victim must first go through a process of healing.

One of the first parts of the healing process for many survivors of violence is to find someone to talk to.

TO TELL OR NOT TO TELL

Sometimes young people hesitate to talk to their parents about their experiences with violent crime. For many reasons, this reluctance is understandable. Some want to spare their parents pain and worry. Some are embarrassed by what happened. Others worry that their parents will be angry with them or won't believe them.

Should you or shouldn't you tell? The question comes up not only in rape cases but in other crimes. Were you hanging out with the wrong crowd when you were assaulted? Had you forgotten to lock your new bike when it was stolen? Did you take something to school you should have left at home? For Greg, one of the worst parts of having his bike stolen was his worry about what his mother would say.

Although telling may be difficult, it is probably best in most cases. Parents may be upset, but they'll get over it, and sometimes they have resources that will help. Young people who have tried to "keep the secret" find the effort emotionally draining. Besides, parents have ways of discovering things even if you don't tell them.

One technique that works well with most parents is to tell them *after* you have taken at least some steps to remedy the situation. If you got in a fight at school, you might tell your parents after you've arranged a meeting to discuss the assault. Mack told his parents after he had earned $35 to replace the stolen baseball glove he knew he shouldn't have taken to school.

One reason that telling someone about the abuse is so important is that specialized therapy can help both the perpetrator and the victim. If someone has victimized you, the same offender has probably done the same to many other victims. By telling, you'll have a chance to help others as well as yourself.

Listening to the Victim

That's what some inmates of the Rikers Island Correctional Institution have been doing. According to the *New York Times* (April 5, 1993), a new program sends crime victims or their relatives into prisons to explain how it felt (and still feels) to be a victim of a violent crime. For example Ralph Hubbard, a retired New York City police officer, told how he lost his twenty-three-year-old son Brett to a shooting in a fight over a videotape. After three months of listening to similar true stories, inmate Charles Thomas said he was touched by the visitors' pain. "It's making me think in new directions," he said.

The aim of the program is to get offenders to see the other side, to make a personal connection between what they do and the people affected by their actions. Brett Hubbard was "a gentle kid" and a gourmet chef. When he was shot, his life had just begun. His family, including three sisters, miss him very much.

Another victim, David Opont, fifteen, lived to tell about the horror of attempted homicide. David was on his way to school three years ago when a boy two years older enticed him into a basement and set him on fire. Burned over half of his body, David had a 50 percent chance of survival. According to the *New York Times* (April 6, 1993), David's attacker was sentenced to three years at a youth residential center.

David's recurring nightmare is that his attacker is coming back to kill him. The once happy young man has become a lonely, angry boy. In spite of his anger and fear, David says he doesn't hate his tormentor. "If I could talk to him, I would tell him to stay away from drugs and to start looking toward his future, because he's got a lot ahead of him."

THE THERAPY EXPERIENCE

Sometimes victims have suffered so much emotional damage that family and friends cannot adequately help them come to terms with their pain. At such a time they may want to turn to an objective person such as a therapist or counselor who can bring a professional point of view to the situation.

How do you get started with a therapist? First, decide whether you would prefer a male or female therapist. Then obtain recommendations from friends, family members, a school counselor, or from your victim/witness assistance office.

Before making any phone calls, check the distance from your home to the therapist's office. Can you afford the expense and time of travel, or can you find someone closer to home? Many questions such as length of sessions or cost can be answered in a telephone call. Many therapists offer one free consultation during which you can make up your mind about continuing. At this time, feel free to ask more questions. Do you specialize in treating people of my age and with my concerns? What is the fee and how is it to be paid? Do you expect my family to come with me? Therapists should inform you of their qualifications.

In the therapy session, client and therapist enter into a contract. The goal is healing. In this relationship, both parties have responsibilities. Some of the duties, such as keeping appointments and being on time, are the same for both. Some responsibilities are parallel but different. For example, the therapist has expertise in helping people with their problems; the client pays a fee for this help. The therapist holds what the client says in confidence; the client in turn speaks freely.

Here are some important things to remember:

- The therapist sets the rules for therapy, but you are free to ask questions about the rules.
- You are working toward a goal, that of healing yourself. The therapist is there to assist you in making your own recovery.
- Be sure to tell the whole truth and nothing but the

truth to the therapist. You are not there to make
the therapist like you or be impressed with you.
You are there for healing.

Reestablishing a feeling of safety may take weeks,
months, or years, depending on the person and the type
of violent crime he or she has endured. During the time
you are seeing a therapist, continue talking with friends
and family.

If your therapist is a psychiatrist (a physician), he or she
may prescribe medication to relieve feelings of anxiety or
depression. If your therapist is a social worker, a member
of the clergy, or a psychologist, he or she may refer you to
a psychiatrist to see if medication would be of value. Your
therapist may give you "homework tasks," such as relaxation techniques or physical exercise. If you can establish a
trusting relationship with a therapist, you will eventually
be able to reestablish trust with other people in your life.

Keep Working

The survivor must feel "safe enough" to be able to tell the
story of the crime in depth. When memories are deeply
buried, as they are in some cases of sexual abuse, the
work of uncovering them can be very hard. Along with
the memories will come a sense of grief and loss.

Many times during this period of remembering, talking,
and then remembering more, victims try to figure out a
reason for what happened to them. Years of physical abuse
by her father caused Peggy to ask, "Why?" and "Why
me?" Peggy needed constant reassurance that what had
happened was not her fault.

Peggy felt powerless. "The worst part," she adds, "is
that I thought no one would rescue me from this disaster."

She also relives the experience in her mind as if it were still happening in the present. "Whenever someone hits me real hard, I suddenly see my father hitting me."

At this stage, the most important thing is to realize that although you were not responsible for the violence, you *are* responsible for getting over it. Taking the responsibility for making your life better *today* will free you to get on with your life.

Onward and Upward

The next stage of healing involves reconciling with yourself and reconnecting with others. Reconciling with yourself includes being able to love yourself. To love yourself, you have to get to know yourself.

You already know yourself? Then see if you can get to know yourself better. One way is to write your autobiography. What do you like best about yourself? What *don't* you like about yourself? Are you willing to change those parts, or will you have to learn to accept them? In making these choices, you are taking control of your own destiny.

Another helpful technique in learning to love yourself is positive self-talk. Throughout the day try countering each of your negative thoughts about yourself with a positive thought. Tess, for example, always put herself down. Her negative words to herself sounded something like this: "Danielle makes me feel bad. She looks at me as if I had asked to be assaulted. She makes me feel as if I have *rape* written on my forehead. She makes me feel like a slime ball!"

When Tess learned to use positive self-talk, her messages to herself sounded like this: "I am the only one who can make myself feel a certain way. I am responsible for my own thoughts and feelings. I choose to feel good about myself because I am a beautiful person. I will take care of myself because I have a lot to offer the world."

Reconnecting with others often requires hard work. After being victimized, you may have chosen to withdraw from life for a while. A little while may have turned into a long time. You may have to rebuild your support networks.

For a starter, make a list of friends and acquaintances, people you see every day or every week. Then make a check mark by the people you trust. Ask yourself why you trust them. Are they good listeners? Do they have ways that make you feel good about yourself? Are they kind to you and to others? Next mark off people who are not helpful. If you have a long list of those and your list of supportive people is small, start reaching out. You may want to begin with just one person. Invite that person to have lunch with you or go out for coffee. Talk honestly. Listen. Do something thoughtful for a friend. Your reaching out may go beyond friends to individual therapy. Or you may decide to join a support group for victims of violence or a 12-step program. Chapter 10 lists a number of organizations you may find helpful.

For Aubrey, age twenty, an eating disorder was one of the aftereffects of sexual abuse by her stepfather. For years Aubrey made secret midnight raids in her parents' kitchen. She hoarded food in her closets and dresser drawers. When she stayed overnight with friends or when she baby-sat, she couldn't resist gorging on anything and everything in her hosts' cupboards and refrigerators. Finally she found herself without friends or work. Long-term individual and family therapy helped get Aubrey's eating disorder under control. She went back to school to become a social worker. Ultimately she got a job in a specialized outpatient clinic helping others with eating disorders.

Some people reconnect by turning their tragedy into an opportunity to help others. Marva and Ron Hicks lost their only son, Theron, to violence. He was gunned down by a sixteen-year-old whose mother had given him the murder weapon. Marva, who dislikes speaking in public, began speaking about guns. Ron speaks too. He scans the faces of the group in front of him and says, "We hurt. We are in grief because our son is gone. If this issue is left unaddressed, the problem will hit *you*." Ron and Marva helped form an organization called PUNCH (Parents United: No Children's Handguns) and are actively working for gun control.

In the stage of reconnection, the survivor of a violent crime spends less time looking back and more time looking at the present and future. One way to look toward the future is to find ways to protect yourself. For instance, you can learn some of the basics of self-defense.

Self-defense is a related group of strategies and physical techniques that help you prevent and resist physical attacks. You learn ways to escape and survive, to be assertive, and to problem-solve.

Model Mugging, one such program that exists in more than twenty cities in the United States, is more than self-defense; it is empowerment. Participants learn that they can be strong, emotionally, mentally, and physically. The program teaches such actions as screaming, punching, and kicking—if possible or practical. Supporters say it's an assertive way to say no to violence. It's a way to recapture the power that someone has tried to take away from you. Check with a local rape crisis center or victim/witness advocate for a list of self-defense classes. Often Ys, community schools, and colleges offer self-defense courses.

Another way of reconnecting is to sign up for planned and supervised encounters with danger, such as wilderness trips, that give you a chance to practice stress reduction and face your fears. During and after such a trip, victims learn to think about protecting themselves. They have to cope and are often surprised at how well they *can* cope. Some wilderness experiences include a "solo" during which participants go out alone and have to rely on themselves. An example is an Outward Bound mountaineering course that teaches such skills as navigation, rope handling, rapelling, and camping. April, an eighteen-year-old, says, "For me this course was a real triumph. I was the smallest person in the group and have always thought my size was a handicap of sorts, but during this trip I proved to myself that I was strong and that my limits were more mental than anything."

Joining a group is another way to reconnect. Groups take many forms; you can try out different kinds and choose the one that feels most helpful. Some therapy groups are led by professionals such as psychiatrists or social workers. Other groups are "self-help." Some are 12-step groups modeled on the principles of Alcoholics Anonymous.

Because a violent crime breaks the bonds of trust, survivors can often reconnect in a group experience with others who have gone through similar kinds of victimization. Groups can be especially helpful for survivors of sexual abuse. An obvious advantage is that the sharing of others helps to end your feelings of isolation: Other group members have been there and have survived. Usually they are wrestling with the same types of problems that are besetting you.

A word of caution: Such a group may not be appropriate immediately after a violent crime. Usually a victim needs to use other healing resources first. Professionals recommend joining such a group about six months down the line.

You don't have to join a *therapy* group. If your goal is simply to get back in touch with people, you might try a group organized around a sport or other interest; try a co-ed volleyball or softball team or a choral group.

Sometimes a noncredit course such as art, music, or writing can turn into a kind of support group. It might be just what you need to get out of a rut. Consider these course titles listed in the catalog of a noncredit university: "Feel the Fear and Do It Anyway: How to Get Your Life Unstuck," "The Gentle Art of Verbal Self-Defense," "Asserting Yourself Positively: Getting What You Want Without Putting Others Down," "Building High Self-Esteem: 10 Secrets of Making You Like Yourself."

RECOGNIZING AND ACCEPTING YOUR EMOTIONS

You need to tune in to your own emotions. Some people go through life as emotional robots; they are unaware of their own feelings and the feelings of others. These people are underdeveloped; they are *deniers*. Oscar stiffens when someone asks him how he's feeling; he doesn't know. He never asks other people about their feelings or shows interest in others. Oscar is like a cube of ice—until someone crosses him. Then he explodes, but he can't understand how he got so mad.

Some people seem angry all the time. They don't *get* angry; they *are* anger. We all know the person with the screeching, thumping boombox or the roaring motorcycle. Sally *always* talks in a loud voice and is constantly enraged about something. Sally *overexpresses* her feelings.

Other people are caught somewhere between the deniers and the overexpressers. They *feel* the emotion but are unable to express it. Some get abdominal cramps and migraine headaches from unexpressed emotions.

Fear

Aaron, seventeen, says, "Don't be afraid, because living in fear is not living at all." And yet those who have been victims of violent crimes have felt fear and will continue to feel fear long after the crime is over.

Actress Theresa Saldana still felt fear, anger, and pain after being stabbed repeatedly by a crazed fan, who said when apprehended that he wanted to send her to heaven. He hoped to be executed for the crime, so he could "join her in paradise."

Fear or terror are normal responses to violent crimes. Trying to rush a crime victim into getting over the fear adds abuse to the abuse of the crime. This "treatment" is like forcing a child who's afraid of the dark into a closet or throwing a child afraid of water into the deep end to help him "get over it."

If you can admit and accept your fear, you take a giant step toward healing. But remember that fear can be contagious. Listening to your description of your experiences may overwhelm some people. They may be so terrified by what happened to you that they are ineffective as comforters. Others may be helpful *because* they share your fears; all of us fear crime. Seek out friends who have the courage and the willingness to listen.

Anger

Anger is another natural emotion, especially in response to a violent crime. Anger shows you are alive and reacting to the injustice you received. At first your rage may be totally unfocused. Because of her injuries, Saldana was unable to kick, cry, scream, or throw things. But these reactions may be totally appropriate and even helpful to some people during the early stages of recovery from victimization.

In *The 12 Step Times*, a journal of addiction, recovery, and personal growth, Dwight Wolter lists *inappropriate* responses to anger. The use of alcohol, drugs, food, risky sex, gambling, and other addictions to try to control anger is harmful and does nothing to solve the problem. In fact, such addictions make the problem worse; they may cause you to "numb out." When you "come to," however, the cycle of self-abuse is likely to start all over again with even more frequency, intensity, and damage. You have not confronted the anger in a healthy way.

Tammy, seventeen, the survivor of a date rape, says, "At first I was scared. Then I felt cheap and used. That feeling made me angry. I turned to drinking, drugs, and not caring."

Expressions of anger that are *not* appropriate include:

- *Violence and bullying.* These ways of dealing with anger harm others and cause the conflict to escalate.
- *Control, manipulation, domination.* These "power plays" are attempts to get someone else to respond like a marionette with you pulling the strings.
- *Dumping and raging.* Think of a dump truck filled with garbage. Do you want to bury someone else with your "garbage"? Some people, says Wolter, get *in* touch with their anger only to discover that they can't get *out* of touch with it.
- *Blaming.* This expression of anger is inappropriate because the victim takes no responsibility for heal-

ing. Taking responsibility is what leads to wellness.

- *Divisive humor based on put-downs.* This kind of "humor" isn't funny. According to humor expert Robert Wells, inappropriate or negative humor is anything that cuts people out, such as racist or sexist jokes. Sarcasm is also inappropriate because it makes someone else the victim of the "joke."

These are only a few of the many inappropriate ways some people express their anger. Can you think of others?

Expressions of anger are *appropriate* if they:

- Lead to healing.
- Tell other people what your needs are.
- Lead you to take positive action.
- Take into consideration the feelings of others.
- Lead to dialogue.

Wendy Collier and Stephanie Sund are both angry, but they have decided to channel their anger to help other victims. These two young stalking victims were brought together by violent acts each endured separately. Wendy and Stephanie have formed a nonprofit business, Victim Protection Services (*Rocky Mountain News*, March 8, 1993). In 1992 Stephanie's former boyfriend shot her outside a police station. Wendy calls Stephanie and herself "bad victims." Why? Because, she says, ". . . we are empowered victims. . . . We're not little mice. We ask questions that make people uncomfortable. A lot of people see us as angry women. Stephanie has the right to be angry about being shot. I have the right to be angry about facing a loaded shotgun. He held me hostage with a loaded shotgun, and he spent a whopping 45 days in jail. Forty-five days." Wendy and Stephanie are two victims encouraging other victims to stand up for their rights.

Pain

Survivors of violent crimes also feel pain. Even if the crime did not cause physical pain, almost all victims suffer emotional pain. Darcy, sixteen, had to deal with the murder of a friend. "My feelings were a jumble of hurt, confusion, and pain," she says. "For a long time afterward, I felt very depressed. I had to drop out of school for a couple of months."

Theresa Saldana found that keeping her mind engaged was one of the best ways to cope with pain. Even when she couldn't get out of bed, she used the telephone to "connect" with friends. She tried to put herself into their reality. Later she exercised in bed, watched TV, read, or had someone read to her. She played cards and board games—anything to divert her mind from the pain.

Nineteen-year-old tennis champion Monica Seles was stabbed in the back on April 30, 1993, at a tournament in Hamburg, Germany. Her assailant was a fan of another player. Seles, who is left-handed, received a one-inch wound in the left side of her back. While coping with pain from the injury, Seles said she would also consider getting psychological help for the emotional pain she suffered. She still had not returned to the tennis tour a year later.

Recovery from a violent crime takes a long time; some victims never feel completely healed. Others emerge from their trauma almost like a butterfly from its cocoon. As a result of their growth, these young people are more mature and more beautiful than they were before.

CHAPTER 5

With Liberty and

Justice for All?

F or some crime survivors, having their loss or injury redressed in a court of law is an important part of healing. Most victims expect justice. What *is* justice? The dictionary defines it as "fair handling; due reward or treatment." In other words, victims expect offenders to be punished. Victims may also expect compensation and special treatment to help make up for the pain they've suffered. Government agencies that enforce laws, prosecute violators, hear charges in court, and punish offenders make up the *criminal justice system.*

The criminal justice system in the United States comes originally from English common law. The system aims to find a suspect for every crime, to decide if the suspect is innocent or guilty, and to punish him if he is guilty. Today many authorities look at our bulging prisons and rising crime rates and wonder if punishment is working.

Justice, when it occurs, often involves *more* pain for the

victim. It may involve long court hearings and delay after delay. Even after much exasperation on the part of the victim, the offender may not get the punishment the victim believes he deserves.

A recent study showed that of every 100 felonies committed in the United States, only 33 are reported to police. Seventeen of these result in arrests, but only three result in conviction. For this and other reasons, many victims do not report crimes.

THE BENEFITS OF REPORTING

If you do report a crime, you give the police a *chance* to catch the offender. You increase the chances for justice. If you expect to receive reimbursement or restitution for your expenses as a crime victim, most states require you to report the crime to police within a week. Obviously, if you do not report, there is no chance of catching the criminal, and he or she is free to victimize again and again.

If you win (the offender is caught and punished for the crime), or even if you lose (the offender is not punished), you will feel a sense of power. You will have the satisfaction of having done all you can do to fight crime and at least *trying* for justice.

Getting over the effects of a violent crime is based on empowerment. Doing something is empowering. In some cases after a long hard battle, victims do achieve success. Dr. Herman says, "By making a public complaint or accusation, the survivor denies the perpetrator's attempt to silence and isolate her, and she opens the possibility of finding new allies."

When Molly testified two and a half years later against the man who had raped her, she was "exuberant and confident. She reveled in the chance to fight back." Before the hearing she said, "I'm excited about testifying, excited about him being convicted."

Making one's way through the criminal justice system can be frustrating. Therefore, it's important to have the support of friends, parents, and other strong adults. Sometimes the system seems responsive, but at other times it does not seem to be of much help to victims. Not until the early 1970s did the needs of crime victims begin to be recognized with the establishment of victim/witness assistance units through local prosecutors' offices. Every state has at least one of these units. Victim/witness programs are discussed later in this chapter.

In 1983, after approximately two hundred years, the Supreme Court began to recognize the rights of crime victims. Although these rights are not guaranteed by the Constitution, the Supreme Court ruled that they should not be ignored. Recently a strong movement has arisen toward creating more programs to empower victims and provide various kinds of assistance. More than half of the states have statements such as the following regarding the rights of crime victims:

- Victims and witnesses have a right to be treated with dignity and compassion.
- Victims and witnesses have a right to protection from intimidation and harm.
- Victims and witnesses have a right to be kept informed about various phases of their case, including investigation, prosecution, trial, and sentencing.
- Victims have a right to provide information and input to the criminal justice process, especially at such key points as plea bargaining, sentencing, and parole hearings.

- Victims have a right to restitution as a condition of sentencing.
- Victims have a right to the speedy return of their property used for evidence.
- Victims have a right to notification from officials about arrest or release of defendants, time and location of legal proceedings or trials, continuances or delays in trial proceedings, sentencing, and parole hearings.
- Victims and families have the right to be informed about eligibility for state crime compensation or financial support, where applicable, and to be helped in completing application forms in a timely manner.

THE ROLE OF THE POLICE

When police officers arrive at the scene of a crime, they must take control. Part of taking control is establishing whether or not a crime is still in progress. The officers check for injured parties and establish a crime scene. They may rope off a certain area. In some crimes, there may not be enough evidence to do much of an investigation. If you leave your car unlocked and someone rips out your tape deck, the police will probably lack evidence. They are not required to investigate every crime. With limited time and human resources, they have to establish priorities. The real investigative work usually begins at the level of burglaries and domestic violence.

When the police do decide to conduct an investigation, collect evidence, and arrest suspects, various officers may be involved. If you report a crime, be sure to write down the names and identification numbers of the officers who talk to you. If you have a case number, record that too.

One of the most important ways to help your case is to be truthful, even if the truth is embarrassing or reveals that you did something you shouldn't have done. In this example, Jasmine's friend could have lied, but if the lie had caught up with her, she would have jeopardized a good chance for conviction of the criminal.

Jasmine, fifteen

"My friend really trusted this guy. He was the best friend of her boyfriend. One night she was unable to find a ride home. Because she trusted this guy, she went with him. He forced her to have sex. My friend was afraid to tell anyone because she wasn't supposed to be there. Eventually [a few months later], she told a counselor at school, and the police caught the guy."

If you meet with a police officer and later remember some further details, be sure to let the officer know. Sometimes writing in a journal or putting thoughts on tape will help you remember.

The police may ask you to help make a drawing of the offender or to look at mug shots or view a lineup. (Mug shots are photos of people who are already on record as having committed crimes. A lineup, held at the police station or district attorney's office, is usually done behind a one-way mirror. You can see the suspect, but he can't see you.) Seeing an offender in a lineup or in court is likely to bring back unpleasant memories. Be sure to have a supportive person with you.

Karen, sixteen

"I was only ten years old when this guy jumped into the car where I was sitting with my younger sister. We were waiting for Mom to come out of a store. The guy started touching me all over and said if I yelled, he would stab me with a knife he had in his pocket. When we got home, Mom called the police.

"About two weeks later, a detective came to the house and asked me to draw a picture of the guy. He said they thought they'd found him, and I'd have to try to pick him out of a lineup. I never had to do that though.

"I don't know how it all turned out. It was embarrassing, because everyone in the neighborhood saw the police at our house, and at the time I didn't feel like telling the whole world what had happened."

As Karen looks back, she appreciates the police department's hard work. But because of her age at the time, her main memory was of acute embarrassment over police involvement in her life.

Sometimes nothing seems to result from the efforts of the victim. It may appear as if the police have done nothing. But the police may not have been able to collect enough evidence to make a case, or the incident may not be considered a crime. So in spite of the fact that you've told your story over and over, no arrest is made. This apparent lack of success can be deeply disappointing.

If we make an effort to understand the difficult and dangerous job of police officers, we may have more sympathy for their work. The job of a police officer is to fight crime. Worrying about the feelings of the victim is not in the job description. In fact, some authorities believe that preoccupation with the emotions of the victim may hinder police effectiveness.

To face the danger and pain in which they find themselves each day, police officers may have to wear (along with their bulletproof vests) an "invisible armor," a shell that protects them from overwhelming emotions such as despair. Many experts believe that without their invisible armor police officers would quit, burn out, or turn into zombies.

THE COURTS

Court proceedings differ greatly in the United States, depending on the crime and where it happened. Also confusing is the fact that physical acts such as rape may be tried in two courts, a *civil court* and a *criminal court*. A civil court requires a lower standard of evidence to prove an alleged act than does a criminal court. A rape victim may sue in civil court (in her name) to recover money damages. In criminal court the *state* (The People) prosecutes to punish the offender, and the case must be proved beyond a reasonable doubt.

Although most of us know that the defendant (the person charged with the crime) is considered innocent until proven guilty, this is a difficult concept for victims, especially if the defendant is freed on bail. (Bail is money given to the court as security or as a promise that the accused person will return to court when called. If the accused does not appear when ordered to do so, a warrant is issued for his or her arrest, and the bail money is forfeited).

The Prosecutor

Reporting a crime does not mean you have to "press charges." Pressing charges is actually a filing done by the prosecutor's office. The prosecutor is an attorney, sometimes called the district attorney (D.A.) or the state's attorney. The D.A. decides what charges will be filed and argues the case before a judge or jury. The prosecutor represents The People because a criminal act is an offense against all of society, not just one person.

Prosecutors do not attempt to try all cases. They may believe that a particular case will not result in a conviction. An arrest may have been made for an act that was not really a crime. Courts sometimes allow an offender to do community service. If the offender completes a specified number of hours, the charges are dropped. Finally, prosecutors may drop a case for political reasons.

Must the Victim Appear at a Trial?

Several preliminary hearings may be held before a trial. If you have to testify at such a hearing, you will be notified in advance.

A *subpoena* is a written order stating the time and place of the hearing at which you must appear. The preliminary hearing is open, so you can take friends or relatives along for support. However, if they have witnessed the crime and are needed to give testimony at the trial, they are not allowed to attend the hearing. After this hearing, the judge decides whether the evidence is sufficient to try the case and what type of crime it should be considered.

Two of the main categories of crimes are *felonies* and *misdemeanors*. A misdemeanor is the less serious of the two. It is punishable by a fine and a term of a year or less in jail. Punishment of a felony is imprisonment, usually in state or federal prison, for more than a year. Depending on the charges, a felony case may go to a grand jury.

The Grand Jury

A grand jury sounds big and scary, and in fact it originally was so named because it is larger than a usual jury, involving a maximum of twenty-three jurors. The other persons present are the prosecutor, who asks you questions, and the court reporter, who records your testimony. Because this is a closed hearing, you may not bring friends. But you do not have to face your assailant or his lawyer. The purpose of the grand jury is to decide whether to formally charge the offender or to dismiss the charges.

If the case is dismissed, you will undoubtedly feel angry. Strategies to deal with anger are discussed in Chapter 4. A first step is getting the prosecutor to explain what happened. Ask questions. The reason for dismissal probably has to do with legal issues. You should not feel as if you have failed in any way.

Plea Bargaining

Many court cases are settled without a trial. They are said to be settled "out of court." One method is called *plea bargaining*. The defendant agrees to plead guilty, but to a lesser charge than the original charge. In return, the prosecutor agrees to reduce the charge. If the judge accepts the plea bargain, a trial may be unnecessary.

The advantages of a plea bargain are that the victim is spared the trauma and publicity of a trial, and society is spared the expense of a trial and the possibility that the prosecutor may not obtain a conviction. In spite of these advantages, victims, police, and others often dislike plea bargaining because it seems to offer the defendant an easy way out.

Witness for the Prosecution

If the case in which you are involved does go to court and you are asked to testify, you will give your testimony as a witness for the prosecution. The prosecutor may meet with you before the trial to help you understand the procedures.

Most people feel intimidated in court. Marie Nielsen, a victim/witness assistance coordinator, says she often takes victims to see the court when it is not in session, to help with "courtroom jitters." If the court is in a big city, however, such a preliminary trip may not be possible.

Often there is a great deal of "hurry up and wait" connected with court. Even something as simple as parking may be a problem, and those familiar with court procedures may not have much patience for those who are not. You may take time off from school or work, only to discover that your case has been postponed. These delays are unavoidable, but they can be upsetting.

The Judge

The job of the judge is to determine the facts of the case. He or she cannot take sides. Sometimes this arrangement may not seem fair to the victim.

After all the witnesses have testifed, the judge (or jury) announces the verdict—guilty or not guilty. If the defendant is found guilty, the judge imposes a sentence at a later sentencing hearing, taking into account such factors as the defendant's previous record. Sometimes the defendant has to pay restitution money to the victim.

JUVENILE COURT

The above overview applies to the adult court system. Because there is no national juvenile justice system in the United States, ways of dealing with young people who commit crimes differ in every state. If the offender is considered a juvenile (usually under age eighteen), the case will probably be heard in juvenile court. Juvenile court is set up in much the same way as adult court. If asked to testify, it is important for you to do so. Without the victim's testimony, there is likely to be no case against the accused.

Derek, fourteen

"*A couple of older guys knocked me and my friend off our bikes. We called the police, who picked up the two guys and got our bikes back. My friend and I wanted to press charges, so we went to juvenile court. Those guys were there sitting with their parents. They both looked like they were about to throw up. Reporting this crime and standing up for myself made me feel great.*"

Young offenders who appear in juvenile court do not end up with a criminal record. The purpose is to protect young people from the stigma of being convicted of a crime. In these days of serious crimes committed by younger and younger people, however, more such cases are being tried in adult criminal court.

The Victim/Witness Assistance Program

From the first scary moments after a violent crime until the case has gone through the court system, you will have questions. You will also feel the need for extra support. The Victim/Witness Assistance Program is designed to give that support to crime victims and to those who have witnessed violence.

Giving emotional support is only one of the services of these special units. Other services include:

- Providing emergency assistance to victims immediately after the crime.
- Providing transportation in crisis situations.
- Giving names and telephone numbers of other agencies that may be able to help the victim.
- Giving victims information on the status of their case as it moves through the criminal justice system.
- Helping victims retrieve their property.
- Giving information about the rights of victims.

You can get this kind of help by asking your police department for information or by looking in the telephone book under Victims' Assistance or Victims' Services Agencies.

If you need further help, try the National Organization for Victim Assistance (NOVA), 1757 Park Road NW, Washington, DC 20010. This organization helps victims get financial compensation, advocates for expanded victims' rights, and finds help for victims with prosecuting and other court-related matters.

Ginny, a young woman raped by a counselor in her group home, received help from the victim/witness assistance program in her city. During the long court process, Ginny's special advocate kept her informed about the progress of her case. "I felt like I finally had a friend in the system," she says. The program also provided money for counseling.

As mentioned earlier, such a friend in the system is Marie Nielsen. She is an out-going, knowledgeable woman who helps victims and witnesses from her small office in the police station in Parker, Colorado. But Nielsen doesn't spend much time in her office. As a bridge between the police department and the criminal justice system, she helps victims of all ages. She and her volunteers contact all victims and witnesses of crimes in the area in person, by telephone, or by letter.

More than half of Nielsen's cases are concerned with family violence. While we usually think of domestic violence as spouse abuse, it can also refer to violence in families or in close family-like relationships. For example, a teenager may call to complain of abuse by a parent, or a parent may complain of abuse by a teenager. From parents, Nielsen often hears something like: "I can't do anything with the kid, and I want him out now."

In such cases, Nielsen may point out the alternatives. A young person can live at home, or on the streets, or be picked up by the police and placed with social services. In the latter instance, a parent must pay for foster care. A knowledge of these alternatives is often enough to send parents and children "back to the drawing board" to try to settle their disputes.

Nielsen considers her department an adjunct to the police department. Although the concept of victim/witness assistance is relatively new, Nielsen says, "The police accept us because they see what a help we can be. We tend to the emotional and informational needs of the victim."

"We tell people we're here for them," adds Nielsen. "Then we help victims help themselves." Nielsen and the thirty volunteers are advocates for victims. They suggest resources, but they don't try to solve people's problems for them. In fact, that wouldn't even be useful.

If a person in a relationship says to Nielsen, "I think I'm being abused. What do I do next?" Nielsen often turns the question back to the person who asked it. "You have a problem," she might say. "What are some things you could do about it?" Although she turns the *question* back, Nielsen doesn't turn *her* back on the victim. Along with Nielsen's counseling, the police do their own independent investigation.

Those who report victimization and follow their case through the criminal justice system are taking the risk that they could lose—again. But each risk taken strengthens the system. If you lose your case and the offender goes free, you will probably have feelings similar to those you had when you were first victimized. If this is your situation or even if you have "won," you need to put all your coping strategies in place.

CHAPTER ◇ 6

Coping with Grief
and Loss

t's amazing how many crime victims say the best way
to cope with a violent crime is to "forget about it."
Impossible. No matter what kind of crime you have
lived through, you will have to do some grieving or
mourning. You may grieve for your loss of innocence or
faith in human nature; you may grieve for the property
someone took from you; you may grieve the loss of family
members or friends. Grieving is hard. No wonder some
counselors call it grief *work*.

Janet, eighteen

*"Last year somebody broke into our house and took a
bunch of stuff. At first I couldn't believe it; then I
was furious. The nerve of those people—breaking
glass that we had to clean up and replace, coming
uninvited into our house, snooping through our*

drawers. They helped themselves to cameras and a disc player, but we can replace those. The worst thing is that they took my grandmother's watch. It didn't even work, but it was all I had to remember her by. She died three years ago. She was always there for me, and I probably didn't pay enough attention to her. I treasured that watch. Now I only have memories. The whole thing makes me really sad. Plus I feel creepy. What if they come back? Well, if it happens, there isn't a whole lot I can do about it."

As the result of a violent crime, Janet is experiencing a whole range of normal grief reactions, the same kind of reactions survivors have when someone close to them dies. First, the victim feels *shock* or *denial*: This couldn't have happened to her. Second, the victim may feel *anger* over something she was helpless to prevent. Janet also feels *guilt* that she didn't pay enough attention to her grandmother and that she is somehow being punished. She feels *panic* too; perhaps the worst is yet to come. Finally, she feels *powerless*.

GRIEF STAGES

A victim may experience some or all of the emotions listed below and may find that some emotions overlap others.

- *Shock.* This feeling is more numbness than emotion. Some describe shock as a fog-like or frozen state in which the victim is unable to handle any more information. Mike had a best friend whose grandmother was shot: "I was shocked. Why would

someone gun down an old lady? They had no right.
I just didn't want to hear about it."

- *Denial.* In denial, the "freeze" continues. Denial is
a coping mechanism that buys the victim time to
get the skills necessary to cope with the "wound."
Aaron's car was stolen from in front of his house.
"My immediate reaction was laughter. I always
made jokes about how no one wanted that hunk of
junk. I never thought it would really happen. I
expected to go back out a few minutes later and see
it sitting there."

- *Hurt.* When the "defrosting" begins, hurt may
result. The victim moves from numbness into feeling, which is often painful. Remember how frozen
fingers and toes feel when they start to warm up?

- *Blaming.* In this stage, a victim may go back to
the beginning of the incident and imagine how he
could have done things differently. This is a way of
trying to assume power in a situation in which you
may have been powerless. Ted, for example, said
he might have tackled the intruder who broke into
his house. When he thought about it, however, he
realized that a thirteen-year-old, especially a small
person like himself, would have had no chance
against a possibly armed "professional" burglar. By
calling 911, Ted had done all he could do.

- *Guilt.* Survivors of a violent incident may feel
guilty because they survived and someone else did
not. One way of dealing with guilt is to make lists:
"What I Could Have Done," and "What I Actually
Did." Comparing the two, you may realize that
you did everything you could.

- *Depression.* Anger not dealt with can turn into a
short- or long-term depression that saps a person's

energy. Sometimes a counselor can be very helpful in coping with depression.

In a normal grief reaction, a person moves through various feelings and eventually arrives at a mental place of *resolution, healing,* or *acceptance.* On the "grief trip," victims may show behavior that is not usual for them. With time and the progression of the process, these same survivors will return to something near their normal behavior. A survivor may never reach complete acceptance, but when a person has fully mourned, it is possible to accept life for its goodness and move on.

GRIEVING DISTURBANCES

Experts who have studied reactions to death report certain behaviors that are similar to survivors' reactions to violent crime. These disturbances include:

- *Withdrawal.* Many people want to talk about what happened, but others want to be left alone. Jane, eighteen, a "partier" since middle school, did not go out of the house the whole summer after she was raped.
- *Hyperactivity.* In an effort to avoid painful feelings, some people lose themselves in a flurry of activity.
- *Sleep difficulties.* As survivors recover, they may sleep a lot. Others have trouble sleeping. Some wake up early. After his house was burglarized, George woke up every day at 3 a.m., imagining he heard noises. Someone's breaking in, he thought. When he looked outside, he saw shadows moving in the moonlight. He couldn't go back to sleep.
- *Eating disorders.* Some victims report an almost

total lack of appetite following a violent incident.
Others use food to make themselves feel better;
they may find themselves eating out of control.
Joyanna gained twenty pounds after she was assaulted and almost raped in the school parking lot.
"It was a comfort to stuff myself," says Joyanna. "I
guess I thought an extra layer of blubber would
protect me."

- *Forgetfulness.* When preoccupied with concerns
  related to the crime or memories of what happened,
  crime victims may find themselves doing silly, for-
  getful things. One morning Kurt tried to figure out
  why, out of 750 students in the school, he got
  jumped in the hall. He didn't even realize what
  he'd been thinking until his mother asked him why
  he'd put the cereal box in the refrigerator and the
  milk carton on the cupboard shelf.
- *Difficulty concentrating.* Related to the above,
  trouble concentrating may result when a person's
  thoughts are focused on court appearances, getting
  even, or keeping safe. Darcy, sixteen, had to drop
  out of school for two months after the death of her
  friend.

If you find yourself doing weird things, consider the
possibility that they may be related to grieving. If you
have some of the grief behaviors mentioned above, first
recognize them as normal. Don't try to get rid of your
pain by drinking, drugging, or other addictive behaviors
that only add pain on top of pain. *Do* let yourself feel the
pain and realize that it won't last forever. Cry. Then cry
some more. Later, cry again.

Mary's husband, a police officer, was killed on duty.
Mary says the emotional pain she endured gave her life

deeper meaning. Her three children were young when her husband died, and her oldest son, Tom, did not accept or mourn his father's death. For years he imagined his father had been kidnapped and would come back someday. Tom later said he thought that if he didn't talk about his dad's death, it would be less real. When Tom was fifteen, his world collapsed. His denial no longer worked. He couldn't function in school or at home. He needed help, and he knew it. The family doctor referred Tom to a therapist, who put him in the hospital and guided him in reliving the events surrounding his father's violent death five years earlier. Crying with sobs that wracked his body not just once but many times, Tom finally was able to grieve. With the help of a school counselor, the psychiatrist, his family, and friends, Tom moved through the mourning process and became a well-adjusted young man.

Helping Someone Who's Grieving

- Understand that grief is a normal reaction to many kinds of changes, even sometimes to positive changes.
- Be there. In other words, be available to listen to a friend or relative who is grieving after a violent crime. Remember that people often don't want advice. What survivors need most is someone who will listen and encourage the expression of thoughts and feelings.
- Use appropriate touch. A hug or a pat on the back may be more comforting than a thousand words.
- Recognize that grief causes difficulties in concentration. The result may be a lowering of accomplishments in school, sports, or social activities.

- If the person wants your help, assist him in setting realistic goals during the grieving period.
- Remember that grief often continues long after other people think it should be over. Grief may, in fact, continue on some level for a lifetime.

FORGIVENESS

To become a survivor, a victim of a violent crime must be able to forgive. The act of forgiveness will undoubtedly seem difficult, maybe even impossible, but it is a necessary step. Those who are unable to forgive risk being eaten alive by their own anger. If you want to be a survivor, you need to forgive in order to free yourself of hurt and pain. Only then will you be able to get on with your life.

Robin Casarjian, author of *Forgiveness*, explains what forgiveness is *not*. Forgiveness is not excusing someone's inappropriate behavior. Violence, aggression, and abuse are totally unacceptable. You do not have to *accept* another's behavior in order to forgive. Forgiveness is not pretending everything is fine when it isn't.

Then how do we learn to forgive as a way of coming to terms with grief? How do we gain inner peace and healing? One way to start learning how to forgive is to practice on neutral gound. Rather than trying to forgive someone who has "done you wrong," start by seeing the innate goodness in total strangers. Suppose someone holds a door open for you. You say "Thank you" and smile. The other person smiles back. In this small exchange, your inner self has connected with the other person's inner self. You realize that not everyone in the world is a criminal bent on hurting others. Perhaps your gesture helps release that person's pain. Casarjian suggests that practicing this kind of understanding of another's soul will help us learn to forgive.

You don't have to go to the person and tell him you forgive him. But you do need to feel forgiveness within yourself. Psychiatrist David Viscott suggests several ways that will help you let go of the hurt and move on:

- Feel the hurt.
- Express the hurt when it happens.
- Understand that the person has hurt you because of some old unresolved hurt of his own.
- Let go of the hurt in your heart.
- If possible, tell the person you are working on forgiveness. Sometimes this can be done in a letter that is written but not sent.

Helping Yourself

Remember that grief comes in waves and sometimes comes when you least expect it. That's normal. After what you've been through, it's okay to feel down for a while. The pain will pass.

Second, reach out and ask for help. Most people want to help but don't know exactly what to do. You know who your best listeners will be. Find them and ask for a listening ear. Tell them you don't need advice; you just need people who will listen and nod their head once in a while.

Third, try to discover one area in your life in which you can take control. Maybe it is looking as nice as you've ever looked in your life—every day. Maybe it is getting the best grades you've ever gotten. Maybe it is getting thirty minutes of exercise every day.

Some victims of violent crime say that they will never trust anyone. Of course, you won't trust everyone and everything, but as you go through the grieving process you will begin to put your trust in those worthy of it—family, friends, a therapist. Regaining a sense of trust is your main goal. Life may knock you down, but you have to get up again . . . and again . . . and again.

CHAPTER 7

Revenge Is Not the Only Way

Most of us have seen the bumper sticker, "Don't get mad. Get even!" But taking revenge does not solve conflict. There is another way. That way is called *conflict management*, a skill people can use throughout life. If you learn some principles of conflict management, you can use them to decrease violence at home, at school, and at work. You can be part of the solution. First, if you are involved in a conflict, remember that you have choices. You can choose to increase the intensity level of the conflict or you can choose behaviors that will lower the intensity. Second, rather than using violence, try to negotiate or "make a deal" with the other person.

The dictionary defines *negotiating* as "arranging or settling by conferring or discussing." Just because we choose to negotiate doesn't mean we don't get angry. Everyone gets angry; anger can be a useful emotion. Anger tells us something is wrong, that we can try to change the circumstances of our lives. And yet all of us have a tendency to think it's not okay to get angry. However, anger turning to violence is not okay. The following are some suggestions on how to resolve a conflict in a nonviolent, nonangry way.

Take a break. Anger is based on the primal reflex of fear, fear that your wants and needs could be jeopardized. But no one can *make* you angry; you choose to get angry based on the situation. Before you react, get away from the anger-causing person or situation for a while. Take a jog, or walk around the block, or take five steps backward. Say to yourself, "I'm really angry, and I need some time to think." Count to 10, 20, or even 100. Take some deep, relaxing breaths. Punch a pillow or a mattress. It works! While you're diffusing your anger in these ways, do some thinking. Consider your role in the conflict. Are you really angry about what happened or about something else? Maybe earlier in the day the coach yelled at you. Or the dog got white hairs on your new black pants. Are you dumping "old garbage" on the other person? When you have answered questions like this and feel somewhat more calm, return to the other person and get ready to . . .

Listen. Bite your tongue or put masking tape over your lips, but whatever you do, don't lash back. Don't try to explain your side of the conflict until the other person has finished explaining his side. In *The Seven Habits of Highly Effective People*, Steven Covey gives as Habit Five, "Seek first to understand, then to be understood." Covey says most people don't listen with the intention of understanding; they are too busy getting ready to talk. After the other person has completely finished what he has to say, don't jump in immediately. Instead try to repeat what you heard him say. Repeating his message accomplishes several things: It buys time for you both to calm down, it shows the other person you *did* listen, it gives him the feeling that you are trying to understand him, and it gives you a chance to find out if you really did hear what he said. Did you hear correctly? If not, when it's time for him to talk, he'll let you know where you made a mistake. If so, what are you both going to do about your problem? Get ready to . . .

Put yourself in the other person's shoes. Can you understand where he was coming from at the time of the incident? Can you feel any of his feelings? If not, try harder. Ask him to talk some more. If you finally can see his point, get ready to . . .

Brainstorm. In brainstorming, both parties can contribute possible solutions. Write a list of the possibilities you both come up with. Then decide which one you both are willing to try. At this point you both should be ready to . . .

Agree to a change. Try your new method of operating for a mutually agreed upon time. One week? Two? At the end of this period you may decide to continue with the same solution or agree to try something new.

During this whole process, keep your voice "low and slow." That doesn't mean you should act unreal or phony. Just don't yell. If you yell, you can be sure the other person will too. If you stay calm, so will your opponent.

Miguel, fifteen

"Before I even made it to school, I got in a fight. That morning my mom had said something mean about my hair. Because of her remark, I was not in the greatest

mood when I left the house. I kicked this kid's butt and broke his arm. I got a ticket for trespassing and assault and battery. I had to pay a fine of $181. Afterwards I felt sorry for what I had done, but by then it was too late.

From all that happened, I learned not to go out and cause problems. It's not worth it. Being in trouble with the law is the worst thing ever. People start looking at you in a different way, and you feel bad about yourself. The best thing is to have respect for yourself. If you do, you'll have respect for others. After I changed my attitude, the other guy and I became friends. His name is Chris."

We don't know exactly what Miguel's mother said to him, but we can guess it came across as a put-down. He used physical violence on an acquaintance and got in big-time trouble. Miguel's story illustrates several important points about conflict and conflict resolution.

1. We all have the potential to be both victim and perpetractor of violence. Miguel's mother came down hard on him, or at least it seemed so to him. In this instance he was a victim. In turn, Miguel victimized someone else. He became a perpetrator of violence.
2. Anger is a common emotion, not bad in itself. But, as mentioned earlier, we all need to find healthy ways to diffuse anger. (The many ways of diffusing anger are similar to the ways of coping with stress). Understanding the cause of your anger is the first step toward handling it in a mature way.

Miguel might have left the house feeling better if, instead of slamming the door in his mother's face, he had said to her, "I'm sorry if you don't like the way I wear my hair, but it is my hair and I only need to please myself. Thanks anyway, Mom." Or he might have given her an even more prominent "I" message: "I like wearing my hair this way, Mom. I feel kind of angry when people give me negative feedback when I haven't even asked for their opinion."

"I" messages (sometimes called "nonblaming" messages) are useful because first they *are* nonblaming; they express *your* needs and feelings; and second, they are assertive and give you a sense of being in control. If Miguel had used "I" messages, he might not have found it necessary to go out and victimize someone.

If a simple affirming statement such as, "I like my hair this way" doesn't get the desired results, you may have to move on to something more assertive. Miguel might empathize with his mother's point of view while sticking to his own: "I know you want me to look nice, Mom, but this hair style is *in*." He might also remind his mother that she had agreed to stay out of his choices in hair style.

When Miguel had made his point, he might have decided to stop talking and give his mother a chance to speak. She might have said something like this: "It isn't *style* I'm commenting on, Miguel. Your hair looks as if you forgot to run a comb through it."

Miguel might then have made a deal. "Okay, Mom, if I comb my hair, will you agree to make no further comments?"

Another way Miguel might have handled his anger that morning would have been to take a careful look at his mother's situation. As a single mother with two boys to support, she held a full-time job while taking night courses to become a nurse. While Miguel and his brother slept, their mother studied. No wonder she was tired and a bit out of sorts in the morning. All of us, including Miguel and his mother, need to work on developing empathy or sensitivity to another's feelings.

On the other hand, Miguel's mother could have handled her stress in a better way and put her comments more positively. Put-downs rarely lead to positive changes. "I think it's about time for you to get a haircut," she might have said. "I'll take you on Saturday, and we can go out for lunch afterward."

3. Your most important quality is self-esteem. Miguel figured out that the best thing he could do for himself was to respect himself. With self-respect comes the respect of others.

4. Learn to take responsibility for your part in a conflict. Reflecting on what had happened, Miguel realized that breaking someone's arm solved nothing and only made matters worse. Sometimes you may have had no part in causing a conflict. In any case, Redford and Virginia Williams in *Anger Kills* suggest reasoning with yourself about anger. Out-of-control anger not only kills others but can kill you. Anger turned inward can cause heart disease, stomach ulcers, headaches, high blood pressure, and other symptoms and diseases. They suggest that when you become aware of hostile thoughts and feelings, you think about what your anger is doing to *you*.

A CHANCE TO NEGOTIATE

In dealing with the conflicts all around us, we have several options: We can become a dictator or we can withdraw. We can fight and retaliate or we can negotiate. Of all the options, negotiation is the option with the best chance of success.

When you negotiate, you have a goal in mind. Sharon and Gordon Bower in *Asserting Yourself* suggest writing assertive "scripts." These scripts are minicontracts in which you (1) *describe* the other person's offending behavior; (2) express your *feelings* about that behavior; (3) specify *changes* you would be willing to contract for; and (4) specify *rewards* you would be willing to provide for adherence to the contract.

Wes, sixteen

"Me and two friends went to a movie. Inside, two kids were talking very loud and being very rude. I told them to shut up. We exchanged some more hostile words. When the movie ended, one of them punched me. I punched him back, and a fight got going. I got a cut over my eye and got taken to jail. The police told me they would drop the charges of disturbing the peace if I apologized to the theater manager. I was lucky to get off without a record."

Wes might have prevented violence by saying to himself, "(1) Some people are talking too loud. (2) I get upset when I can't hear the movie. (3) If people will just be a little more quiet, (4) I won't have to go to the manager. (5) If they don't quiet down, I will go to the manager and let him or her handle this situation. (6) Then I can enjoy the movie."

Eddie, fifteen

"One day some little punk racists came after me and my friend with baseball bats. We picked up some

rocks and ran, but they caught up with us. At the last minute, they must have gotten scared because they only ended up shouting at us. Sometimes I find myself not liking white people, and this attitude is making me feel more violent toward people in general. My mother told me if I ever see them again, I should put the hurt on them."

Eddie and his mother are reacting with the only weapons they can think of: an eye for an eye, a tooth for a tooth, violence for violence. Is there any other way? Eddie could have stopped and said, "(1) I don't like being chased by armed people. (2) When I see someone who is armed coming at me, I feel angry and violent. (3) If you put down the weapon, (4) we'll agree to drop these rocks. (5) Then we can go our separate ways peacefully."

COPING WITH BULLIES

With some people, no matter how hard you try, negotiating won't work. School authorities are beginning to realize that bullies do not respond to negotiation. Experts estimate that bullies (female as well as male) make up about 15 percent of school populations.

How do you recognize a bully when you see one? Here are a few characteristics:

- Bullies crave dominance and enjoy wielding power over others.
- Bullies lack compassion for the feelings of others; they like to cause pain.
- While their victims may get excited and upset, bullies stay calm.

- Bullies are impulsive; they tend to act without thinking.
- Bullies often blame the victim.

Beverly Title, an expert in conflict management, tells of one bully who "sliced" a woman's arm in a purse-snatching attempt, then blamed her for carrying a purse with a long strap.

Neither standing up to a bully nor negotiation will work. When confronted by a bully, you should report the behavior to an authority who can help. The bully himself may have received physical, sexual, or emotional abuse. Help includes teaching the bully to empathize (understand and appreciate the feelings of the victim) and setting consequences for bullying behavior. One study showed that some bullies who were moved to another school actually stopped their bullying behavior.

STOP VIOLENCE; START SOMETHING

The National Crime Prevention Council reminds us that much violence is preventable. One person, even a young person, can get the ball rolling on a needed crime prevention program. Often one person *can* make a difference. Here are some things you can do.

- Teams of young people with paint and rollers can remove graffiti from buildings and homes in their community. Some groups of neighbors have set up observation posts to watch for graffiti-sprayers; others watch for car thieves and bag snatchers. When they see action, they call police.
- Be a good role model for younger people. Settle

arguments without violence. Use words, not fists or weapons. Stay away from alcohol and drugs and from people and places associated with them. Volunteer to work with a younger person at risk.
- Report crimes and suspected illegal activities to parents, school authorities, and police. Don't be afraid to testify in court, if necessary.

If you want information about organizing to protect your community through a neighborhood crime watch, write Los Angeles Police Department, Devonshire Division, 10250 Etiwanda Avenue, Department P, Northridge, CA 91325. If you want information about organizing an anti-crime group, write Neighborhood Anti-Crime Center, Citizens Committee for New York City, 305 Seventh Avenue, Department P, New York NY 10001.

These are only a few of the ways you can help prevent crime. Can you think of others?

CHAPTER 8

How to Be Safe in an Unsafe World

Most of us give some thought to violent crime and worry about how to protect ourselves. Often people are at either one extreme or the other. The first extreme is thinking it can't happen to you. No matter where you live, a violent crime *can* happen to you. In fact, people who live in high-crime areas are often *safer* than those who live in areas perceived to be crime-free because they take precautions.

Here are some examples of dangerous thinking:

- "We've always left our door unlocked, and we've never had any problems."
- "I don't have to lock my car door in my own driveway."
- "I have good instincts. I can tell by looking if a person is honest or not."

At the other extreme are people who are determined to blame themselves even when they've done nothing wrong.

- "I shouldn't have gone out at night."
- "We should have had a burglar alarm."
- "I shouldn't have taken a purse."
- "Even though I was only in the store for a minute, I should have locked my bike."
- "Mom shouldn't have left us with that baby-sitter."

DON'T BLAME YOURSELF

You've heard it before, but let's hear it one more time: It wasn't your fault. Blaming yourself does nothing to help and may keep you stuck. How can you get out of the quicksand of blaming and start putting what happened behind you? How can you live in the present and look forward with hope to the future?

We are all human; all humans make mistakes. Sometimes these errors increase a person's chances of becoming a victim of random crime. Patricia Harmon in *The Danger Zone: How To Protect Yourself From Rape, Robbery, and Assault*, writes that The Danger Zone is a time and a place in which you are most open to a violent attack. How many times, Harmon asks, have you entered The Danger Zone? Sometimes you may have taken a chance and gotten away with it. At other times you may have gambled and lost. But if you have learned from your mistakes and have gotten on with life as a wiser person, you have won an important battle.

Personal security expert Louis Mizell says that 90 percent of criminals use deception. Their goal is to fool you. If you recognize a trick and refuse to fall for it, you have a good chance of coming out a winner. If they succeed in tricking you, they win.

Sometimes you will find that you did nothing wrong. You made no mistakes, and yet you became a victim of a violent crime. In these instances, you have to accept the fact that evil is random. You just happened to be in the wrong place at the wrong time.

WHAT CAN *YOU* DO?

There are ways you can increase your chances of safety:

At Home

1. Keep doors locked at all times.
2. Do not open the door to strangers.
   a) If someone says he has car trouble and asks to use the phone to call a tow truck, either say your phone is out of order or offer to take the telephone number and make the call yourself. (Don't assume that if the person is female, it's okay to let her in!)
   b) If someone says he has a package to deliver, tell him to leave it on the porch or on the doorstep.
   c) If you're baby-sitting and someone says he has come to make a repair, unless you have specific instructions from the parents, say that you are not authorized to accept the repair.
   d) If two or three policeman flashing badges appear at your door, don't open the door. Instead call police headquarters to see if officers were actually dispatched to your home.
3. Whether you are at your home or at someone

else's hourse, always know exactly what number
to call in case of emergency. Have the telephone
numbers of police, parents, and close neighbors
readily available.

4. If you answer the phone, do not give out personal
information.
   a) Do not let the caller know you are alone.
   b) If the caller asks to speak to an adult, say that
      your parents are busy and do not wish to be
      disturbed. Offer to take a message.

5. If you are in your house or someone else's house
and you hear glass breaking or other strange
noises, call the police immediately.

6. If you come home to find broken glass or broken
door locks, do *not* go inside. Run as fast as you
can to a neighbor's house and call the police.

7. If you are in bed at night and you see someone
in your bedroom, do not confront the person.
Pretend you're asleep.

8. If possible, keep a dog and let it have the run of
the house.

Note: An overwhelming number of authorities do *not*
recommend keeping a loaded gun in the nightstand for
self-defense. The gun is most likely to be used by the
intruder to shoot you or be involved in the accidental
shooting of a child or other family member.

In and Out and Roundabout

In general, especially in big cities, many people do not
feel safe. Almost half of American men limit the places
they go to alone; two thirds of American women do not
feel safe walking alone in their own neighborhoods at
night.

How do you get safely from one place to another? Grace Hechinger writes in *How to Raise a Street-Smart Child* that some kids look "muggable" (spaced-out or unaware of their surroundings). Mugging, she says, means "any unpleasant confrontation in which there is at least the implied threat of bodily harm." No one wants to look muggable or get mugged. Always try to appear alert and "with it."

David, fifteen

David insisted on wearing his stereo headphones whenever he walked the dog, rode his bike, or walked to the bus stop on his way to school. He took pride in ignoring his mother's words, "David, please don't wear those earphones. You can't hear what's going on around you."

That's true, thought David. I can't hear what she's saying, and I don't want to. He told one of his friends that his mother was "an overcautious kook."

One Saturday morning in July, David put the proceeds of a month of lawn jobs in his wallet. He listened to his favorite tunes. His head was in the clouds a thousand miles from nowhere. A pickpocket lifted David's wallet out of his back pocket. Dave didn't even miss it until he started to pay for his new baseball glove. Then he discovered he had no wallet and no money.

Try not to appear too rich or too well-off. If possible, don't carry a purse, especially not one with a long shoulder strap. Tight-fitting backpacks or fanny packs are better choices. Carry keys and ID separately.

More Tips for the Street-Smart

1. Whenever possible, travel in a group or at least with one other person. If you go jogging or walk the dog, don't wear your stereo headset.
2. Right now, figure out the safe places to which you can run if necessary—to a neighbor's house, a gas station, a store. Also, know where public phones are located along your route.
3. Do not take shortcuts though alleys, abandoned buildings, or vacant lots.
4. If a stranger asks you for the time, for matches or cigarettes, or for change, shake your head and keep going.
5. Always let someone at home know where you're going and when you'll be back.
6. As much as possible, keep money, bus pass, watch, and other possessions out of sight.
7. If someone snatches your money, purse, wallet, or other belongings, let them go. Most things are replaceable. You are not. Call the police immediately with a specific description of the offender. Try to observe and remember such things as height, weight or body build, sex, race, complexion, and birthmarks. If a car is involved, get the make and license number.
8. Whenever possible, wear long pants and flat shoes. Women in skirts or dresses and high heels have more trouble escaping.
9. Try to keep one arm free, not filled with books or packages.
10. If a stranger tries to follow you into an elevator, don't go in. Get out and wait for the next one, or take the stairs.

11. Trust your instincts. If you feel something is wrong, it probably is. Don't delay. Get help.

Your Safety ABCs

In summary, here are your ABC (and DEF) rules for conducting yourself safely on the streets of Wherever, USA:

A. *Always Be Alert.* Being aware of your surroundings will discourage offenders, will help you think and act quickly in an emergency, and will help you come up with an accurate description for the police.

B. *Be Loud* (or *Be Quiet*). Some authorities say that if attacked, you should make a lot of noise. Some people carry a metal whistle around their neck or in an easily accessible pocket. Rather than yelling "Help!" some suggest yelling "Fire!" People seem more willing to respond to the latter. Other experts advise talking to the mugger or potential rapist in a calm voice to see if you can get him to leave without hurting you.

C. *Carry Yourself with Calmness and Confidence.* A self-assured stance can be a great deterrent to violent crime. Most criminals are unsure, insecure people who prey on those they perceive as weak.

D. *Don't Battle for Your Property.* And *don't* be ashamed to try to get help. When in doubt, call the police.

E. *Everyone Is Vulnerable.* No matter how tough you look or act, you can still be a victim. Keep this in mind and act accordingly.

F. *Fear Is Useful. Fights Can Kill.* Use your fear to call up some common sense. In other words, decide quickly what is best for you. If that means giving up a valuable possession to save your life, which would you rather have?

Should I Carry a Weapon?

No. Studies have shown that a weapon is most likely to be used *against* the person carrying it.

What If Someone Is Following Me?

Do everything you can to shake the stalker. If you are walking, cross the street and walk faster. Run to the nearest populated area. Try waving and calling out greetings to an imaginary friend: "Hold on, John. I'm coming." If driving, make turns and check in the rear-view mirror. Head for a gas station, a police station, a fire station, or a store. Do *not* go home.

What If Someone Confronts Me on the Street?

1. If there is no way to avoid a suspicious-looking person, start talking. "Don't I know you?" Alexis asked a male who pressed up against her in a quiet bus terminal. "I'm sure my brother went to school with you. He told me he knows you. He thinks you're great. I'm going to tell my brother I saw you." While she talked, Alexis gradually backed away and finally escaped.
2. Potential victims have surprised attackers by quick moves, such as dumping their valuables on the ground in front of the mugger or rapist.

3. Don't put ideas into anyone's head. For example, don't say, "Please don't take my wallet with a hundred dollars inside."

How to Be Safe in Buses or Subways

1. If you are waiting for a bus or other form of public transportation, keep alert. Try to find a well-lighted place to wait. Don't stand in a dark, isolated shelter or doorway.
2. Sit in a populated car close to the driver, or pick an aisle seat for a quick getaway.
3. On a bus or train, don't sit next to an exit door or put your things in an empty seat. Hold your purse or packages firmly in your lap and don't let yourself fall asleep.

Safety Tips for Drivers and Riders

1. Do not pick up hitchhikers and don't *be* one. If you get into a stranger's car or let a stranger in your car, you are imprisoned. If you are driving, a stranger can force you to do whatever he wants. If the stranger is driving, he can take you anywhere.
2. Always lock your car. Drive with locked doors and closed windows.
3. Park in a lighted place, such as a mall lot, rather than in an alley, wooded area, or dark underground garage.
4. If you leave a party or other late-night gathering, always take someone with you to your car. Check inside your vehicle before getting in. Have your car keys firmly in hand. Drive away as soon as possible.

5. Always be sure you have plenty of gas, and keep your car in good working order.
6. If you do have car trouble:
   a) Stay in your car.
   b) Try to keep the car moving. (If you have a flat tire, drive carefully until you get to a place of help.)
   c) Try to summon help. Use your hazard lights or get somewhere from which you can call a towing company or AAA. A car phone would be useful.
7. Drive in the center lane.
8. If someone bumps you from behind, don't get out of your car. Motion to the driver who hit you, then drive to the nearest populated area or police station.
9. If an unmarked police car tries to pull you over in an isolated area, ask yourself if you did anything wrong. If not, drive to a populated area. (The unmarked car may not be a police car.)
10. If someone (a carjacker) tries to take your car, let him have it. Don't risk your life for someone who gets turned on by violence.

CHAPTER ◇ 9

Be Kind to Yourself

One of the most important things to learn when trying to emerge from victim to survivor status is how to take care of yourself. This skill is called *self-nurturing*. Sometimes young people believe they can help themselves by turning to alcohol, cigarettes, or drugs as a way to ease emotional pain, but addictive substances are destructive and only lead to more pain.

The following are a few suggestions you might want to put on your "do" list. Choose activities that appeal to you. See if you can think of other self-nurturing activities to add to your personal list. For discussion purposes, these activities are arranged in three categories—physical, mental/emotional, and other. In reality the various categories overlap.

PHYSICAL

Regular Exercise. One of the best ways to pull yourself out of a low mood is to treat yourself to thirty minutes of exercise every day. Sometimes it's hard to get started on a regular exercise program. If that is a problem for you, schedule your exercise the same way you schedule lunch. Then put yourself on "automatic pilot." If you decide to lift weights at 6:30 a.m., do it whether or not you feel up to it. Soon you will feel so good after your exercise sessions, you'll leap out of bed every morning raring to go.

Be sure to choose exercise you like. Liking it increases your chances of getting it done. Some people are born fish; other people hate getting wet. If you dislike water, don't try to make yourself into a swimmer. Try jumping rope instead. If you need more alone time, try a solitary exercise such as jogging. If being with other people energizes you, try to find someone to bike or hike with. If you miss a day, don't feel guilty. Schedule yourself for the next day and turn on your automatic pilot.

Alternate Forms of Exercise.   T'ai chi and yoga are two of many forms of exercise that increase body flexibility and relieve stress. Courses in these and other alternative forms of exercise are available at recreation centers and community schools.

Massage.   Touch is one of our most important senses. Many people find massage a useful part of healing. Kelsey's grandmother gave her a gift certificate for two massages after someone knocked her down in a purse-snatching incident.

If you can't afford a massage with a certified massage therapist, give yourself a massage or trade massages with a friend.

Relaxation/Meditation.   If you've been a victim of a violent crime, you may notice a tense, uptight feeling in your mind and body. You need to make a conscious effort to put on the brakes and relax. Schedule your relaxation/

meditation time the way you make time for exercise. There's nothing mysterious about relaxation/meditation. Find a comfortable place free of noise and distractions. Lie on your back. Close your eyes. Take a deep breath. Breathe in slowly. Hold it. Now breathe out slowly. Get rid of tension and bad feelings with that breath. Do the same sequence again. Breathe in for a count of three; breathe out for a count of three. Keep out distracting thoughts and worries.

Rituals. Any of the above items can become rituals. Rituals are things we like to do, that add meaning to our lives, and that we do with regularity. If you don't have any self-nurturing rituals in your daily schedule, try some. You might make a ritual around your swimming by taking a long shower afterward and oiling your dry skin. You can add ritual candles to your meditation. One young woman whose house had been burglarized decided to make a daily ritual of burning incense in each room while repeating a blessing for her home.

Nurturing Your Senses. Another way to be kind to yourself is to nurture your senses. Too often we walk around like zombies, unaware of what's going on. Wake up and live! *Smell* the roses, nurture yourself with incense, or inhale the aroma from a cup of herb tea. *See!* Imagine yourself unable to see. Then use your sense of sight with more appreciation. Check out the shape of a cloud, go to a museum, or watch a movie you liked when you were a little kid. *Hear* healing music, listen to bird sounds, listen to silence. *Touch.* Feel the sting of a cold shower, plant something and let the soil flow through your fingers, pet an animal, hug a friend. *Taste!* Make yourself a special treat. Try a comfort food such as a cup of hot chocolate or a bowl of oatmeal. Don't gorge; just enjoy each sip or bite.

Make Your Own Space Yours.   If you spend a lot of time in your bedroom, make it a place you enjoy. Paint, hang posters and pictures of friends. Put up some of your baby pictures. Nurture some plants. Make your room *your* place, a place that will nurture you.

MENTAL/EMOTIONAL

Reframing.   Reframing is finding an alternative way of looking at old problems. Imagine a watercolor of a sunset. The picture is pretty, but you hardly notice it because you are distracted by its ugly broken frame. Imagine the same scene with a golden antique frame surrounding it. A whole different picture!

You can do the same thing with yourself and your problems. Are you accustomed to thinking of yourself as a loser? Do you consider yourself a person who attracts bad happenings? Maybe at times you tell yourself that you deserved to be assaulted; you're just a bad person. For a change, try thinking of yourself as a *good* person. Consider how much you've learned as a result of your experience with the criminal justice system. Think of all the people who came to your aid. Perhaps as a result of that experience you've changed your career direction. Reframing changes your perceptions of yourself and of the world; reframing helps you live in the present and the future instead of in the past.

Living in the Moment.   One of the best ways to be kind to yourself is to live in the *now.* Forget the "if onlys." If only I hadn't gone to that party . . . If only I had locked

the back door . . . If only I could go back and start over . . .
In the first place, you can't go back. Second, this way of
thinking and living is an unhappy state of affairs. Third,
living in the land of "what ifs" keeps you from moving
forward and getting on with your life. Instead, live in the
moment. Concentrate on what you're doing now. Try this:
Isn't this a beautiful day? I'm glad to be alive. This piece
of cake is delicious. I look forward to new challenges. Get
the idea?

Humor. If you want to do something good for yourself,
try laughing.

- Read the comics or books that make you laugh.
- Watch funny movies. Lighten up.
- Put some of your baby pictures on your bedroom
  walls and start calling yourself funny nicknames.
- Try a practical joke on someone who can take it.
- Make a list of ten fun things you've always wanted
  to do. Go do one of them.

Keep a Journal. For some people, writing in a journal
every day is hard work. For others it is fun and becomes
an important ritual. Your journal can be a good place not
only to write but to draw, sketch, or doodle. If you can't
write or draw something in your journal every day, don't
worry. Use your journal as you need it.

Goals. It's important to have realistic goals. Trying to
achieve goals gives a survivor a reason for getting out
of bed every morning. Kate was the victim of a purse-
snatching. For weeks after the incident, she wouldn't
leave the house. Leaving home for only an hour became
Kate's major short-term goal. Finally she was able to

accomplish the long-term goal of going into a crowded place. This time she carried her money and her glasses in a fanny pack.

Affirmations.   Affirmations are positive messages to oneself. Some people combine affirmations with their exercise or relaxation. Saying affirmations over and over is a way to stop putting yourself down with negative messages. Replace negative self-talk with positive messages. Eventually you'll begin to believe yourself. Try saying, "I am strong" over and over. Or say, "I am good. I am good. I am good."

OTHER

Nurturing Others.   Helping someone else can actually bring benefits to *you*. It makes you feel valuable and gives you a mission in life. Put more than the minimum effort into doing a job; go the extra mile. Marianne had a regular baby-sitting job with two preschool children. She began thinking of herself as Mary Poppins. She packed a basket with special toys, markers, paints, and clay. She had fun, and the children were delighted. Jack volunteered to shovel snow for an elderly neighbor.

Spiritual Nurturing.   Whether you believe in a Higher Power or not, whether you go to religious services or not, you have a spiritual base. All people have a center of goodness inside them, which is their spirituality. You can nurture this center by listening for its voice. If you can't hear the voice, try one or all of these suggestions: Be alone for a few minutes; listen to the silence. Try meditation. Get back in touch with nature. Visit a church or synagogue, or visit several. Read a book of philosophy.

Write a poem or a short story. Illustrate it. Give yourself spiritual affirmations such as, "I am a loving person." Many young people have found their spiritual beliefs to be their single most important lifeline.

CHAPTER 10

Where to Go for

Help

I f you have been the victim of a violent crime, the following organizations may be of help to you. Those whose relatives have been victimized may also find some of these organizations helpful.

AIDS Referral
1620 Eye Street NW
Washington, DC 20006
Publishes a national directory of AIDS groups. Important for victims of rape.

Al-Anon Family Group Headquarters
1372 Broadway
New York, NY 10018
A 12-step program for friends and relatives of persons with alcohol-related problems.

Alcoholics Anonymous
P.O. Box 459, Grand Central Station
New York, NY 10163
A 12-step program for those who have problems with alcohol.

American Association of Suicidology
2459 South Ash Street
Denver, CO 80222
For those affected by another's suicide.

Coalition to Stop Gun Violence
P.O. Box 96052
Washington, DC 20077
Works to persuade lawmakers to pass strict gun-
 control legislation.

Emotions Anonymous
P.O. Box 4245
St. Paul, MN 55104
For those with emotional problems.

Families Anonymous
P.O. Box 528
Van Nuys, CA 91408
For friends and relatives of young people who have
 problems caused by drug abuse.

Handgun Control, Inc.
1225 Eye Street NW
Washington, DC 20005
Works to keep handguns out of the wrong hands.

Incest Survivors Anonymous
P.O. Box 5613
Long Beach, CA 90805
A 12-step program for incest survivors.

Narcotics Anonymous
P.O. Box 9999
Van Nuys, CA 91409
For those trying to recover from drug-abuse
 problems.

National Association for Crime Victims' Rights
P.O. Box 16161
Portland, OR 97216
Tries to reverse the overconcern for criminals' rights at the expense of victims' rights.

National Coalition Against Domestic Violence
P.O. Box 15127
Washington, DC 20003
Provides support services for battered women and children.

National　Depressive　and　Manic-Depressive Association
Merchandise Mart
P.O. Box 3395
Chicago, IL 60654
For those suffering from depression and their families.

National Foundation for Depressive Illness, Inc.
P.O. Box 2257
New York, NY 10116
Provides referrals to support groups for those with depression.

National Institute of Victimology
2333 North Vernon Street
Arlington, VA 22207
Works to improve victim/witness services.

National Mental Health Association
1021 Prince Street
Alexandria, VA 22314
Advocates for mental health services.

National Organization for Victim Assistance
1757 Park Road NW
Washington, DC 20010
Works for victims' rights.

National Victim Center
309 West 7th Street
Fort Worth, TX 76102
Promotes public awareness, judicial responsiveness, and prevention techniques for crime victims.

Parents Anonymous
520 South Lafayette Park Place
Los Angeles, CA 90057
For abusive or potentially abusive parents.

Parents United
P.O. Box 952
San Jose, CA 95108
For abused children and adults abused as children.

Phobia Society of America
133 Rollins Avenue
Rockville, MD 20852
For those who suffer from panic/anxiety attacks or phobias.

Protection, Awareness, Response, Empowerment (pre-PARE)
25 West 43rd Street
New York, NY 10036
Teaches IMPACT self-defense and gives emotional support to victims.

Survivors of Incest Anonymous
P.O. Box 21817
Baltimore, MD 21222
A 12-step program for survivors of incest.

Victims of Crime and Leniency
Box 4449
Montgomery, AL 36103
Seeks to ensure that crime victims' rights are recognized
  and protected.

Victims of Incest Can Emerge Survivors
P.O. Box 148309
Chicago, IL 60614
Assists victims of incest.

Glossary

accused   Formally charged but not yet tried for committing a crime.

acquaintance rape   Forced sexual intercourse or other forced sexual acts between people who know each other.

addiction   Habitual or compulsive use of a substance.

affirmations   Positive messages to oneself.

assault   Willful attempt or threat to inflict injury on another person. An assault may be committed without actually touching, striking, or doing bodily harm.

bail   Amount of money set by a judge for pretrial release from custody.

battered woman's syndrome   Term for domestic violence perpetrated against women.

bigotry   Attitude of intolerance or prejudice in politics, race, religion, or other matters.

burglary   The act of illegally entering or trying to enter a place of business or residence. Also called *breaking and entering*. Burglary can be done with force or without force, usually with the intent to steal.

carjacker   Thief who attacks drivers and steals vehicles.

civil court   Court that hears cases concerned with the alleged violation of civil law; not a criminal court.

conflict management   Solving of problems and building relationships through negotiation and communication.

conviction   Judgment of the court that the accused is guilty of the crime for which he or she was tried.

criminal court   Court that hears cases concerned with alleged violations of criminal law.

criminal justice system   Government agencies charged with law enforcement and prosecution of alleged violations of criminal law.

custody The state of being detained or held under guard.

date rape Forced sexual intercourse or other sexual acts between a couple on a date.

defendant Person formally charged with committing a crime.

domestic violence Violence among people in close relationships.

empathy Sensitivity to the feelings of others.

ethnicity Characteristics of a religious, cultural, racial, national, or ancestral nature.

felony A grave crime subject to serious penalties.

grand jury Body of citizens of varying number selected by law and sworn to investigate criminal activity.

homicide The killing of a person by another person without excuse or justification.

jury Group of men and women selected by law and sworn to determine the facts of a case by listening to testimony.

jurisdiction The territorial range of authority and control; the right and power to interpret and apply the law.

larceny Stealing, other than car theft, that does not involve force or illegal entry. Pickpocketing is an example of larceny.

lineup Group of people viewed by a victim or witnesses for the purpose of identifying the person who committed a crime.

manslaughter Causing the death of another person unintentionally but because of recklessness or gross neglect (involuntary or negligent manslaughter) or causing the death of another person intentionally with extreme provocation (voluntary or nonnegligent manslaughter).

mediation Private, informal dispute resolution in which a neutral third party, the mediator, helps parties reach agreement.

misdemeanor Crime less serious than a felony, usually punishable by imprisonment for less than a year.

mugging Assault with robbery as the main motive.

murder Intentionally causing the death of another person without extreme provocation or legal justification; causing the death of another person while committing or attempting to commit another crime.

negotiation The process of submission and consideration of offers until an acceptable offer is made and accepted.

perpetrator Person who commits a crime.

plea bargain Agreement between a prosecutor and a defense attorney that the person charged with a crime will plead guilty to a lesser crime in exchange for a concession.

pickpocketing Theft from a victim by stealth (without the use or threat of force).

prosecutor Person who initiates and carries out legal action on behalf of crime victims. Also called *district attorney* or *state's attorney*.

psychiatrist Licensed medical doctor trained in the diagnosis, treatment, and prevention of mental illness.

psychologist Person with a master's degree, five more years of postgraduate study, and a year of internship geared toward treating mental problems.

rape Sexual intercourse or attempted sexual intercourse by a male with a female other than his wife by force or without legal or factual consent.

restitution The act of restoring to its rightful owner something that has been taken away.

rituals Regularly followed procedures.

robbery The physical taking of property in the possession of another.

sexual harassment Unwanted and unreciprocated sexual attention.

social worker Person trained to help others.

stalking Pursuing or following another person in a stealthy, furtive, or persistent way.

stress Mentally or emotionally disruptive influence.

subpoena Written order requiring a person to appear in a specific court at a specific time and place.

suspect Person believed to have committed a certain crime but not yet been formally charged or arrested.

t'ai chi Ancient Chinese system of exercises for relaxation, meditation, and improved posture.

testimony Statements made under oath in court.

trauma Wound or emotional shock that causes substantial damage to psychological development.

trial Examination of issues of fact and law before a judge or a jury.

For Further Reading

Austern, David. *The Crime Victim's Handbook: Your Rights and Role in the Criminal Justice System*. New York: Viking Penguin Inc., 1987.

Backman, Dr. Margaret. *Coping with Choosing a Therapist*. New York: Rosen Publishing, 1993.

Bard, Morton, and Sangrey, Dawn. *The Crime Victim's Book*. New York: Basic Books, 1979.

Benedict, Helen. *Recovery: How to Survive Sexual Assault for Women, Men, Teenagers and Their Friends and Families*. New York: Doubleday & Company, 1985.

Bower, Sharon and Gordon. *Asserting Yourself: A Practical Guide for Positive Change*. Reading, MA: Addison-Wesley Publishing Company, 1980.

Casarjian, Robin. *Forgiveness: A Bold Choice for a Peaceful Heart*. New York: Bantam Books, 1992.

Covey, Stephen. *The Seven Habits of Highly Effective People: Restoring the Character Ethic*. New York: Simon and Schuster, 1989.

Garbarino, James; Dubrow, Nancy; Kostelny, Kathleen; and Pardo, Carole. *Children in Danger: Coping with the Consequences of Community Violence*. San Francisco: Jossey-Bass Publishers, 1992.

Hechinger, Grace. *How to Raise a Street Smart Child: The Complete Parent's Guide to Safety on the Street and at Home*. New York: Facts on File Publications, 1984.

Herman, Judith. *Trauma and Recovery*. New York: Basic Books, 1992.

Kelly, Liz. *Surviving Sexual Violence*. Minneapolis: University of Minnesota Press, 1988.

Landau, Elaine. *Teenage Violence*. Englewood Cliffs, NJ: Julian Messner, 1990.

Lerner, Harriet. *The Dance of Anger*. New York: Harper and Row, 1984.

Louden, Jennifer. *The Woman's Comfort Book: A Self-Nurturing Guide for Restoring Balance in Your Life*. Harper San Francisco, 1992.

McKay, Matthew; Rogers, Peter; and McKay, Judith. *When Anger Hurts: Quieting the Storm Within*. Oakland, CA: New Harbinger Publications, 1989.

Meltzer, Milton. *Crime in America*. New York: Franklin Watts, 1990.

Miller, Maryann. *Coping with Weapons and Violence in Your School and on Your Streets*. New York: Rosen Publishing Group, 1993.

Mizell, Louis, Jr. *Street Sense for Women: How to Stay Safe in a Violent World*. New York: Berkley Books, 1993.

Nourse, Alan. *Teen Guide to Survival*. New York: Franklin Watts, 1990.

Prothrow-Stith, Deborah. *Deadly Consequences*. New York: HarperCollins Publishers, 1991.

Ray, Veronica. *Choosing Happiness: The Art of Living Unconditionally*. New York: HarperCollins Publishers, 1991.

Reiss, Albert, and Roth, Jeffrey, eds. *Understanding and Preventing Violence*. Washington, DC: National Academy Press, 1993.

Rench, Janice. *Family Violence: How to Recognize and Survive It*. Minneapolis: Lerner Publications Company, 1992.

Saldana, Theresa. *Beyond Survival*. New York: Bantam Books, 1986.

Viscott, David. *Emotionally Free: Letting Go of the Past to Live in the Moment*. Chicago: Contemporary Books, 1992.

Warner, Carmen, and Braen, G. Richard. *Management of the Physically and Emotionally Abused: Emergency Assessment, Intervention, and Counseling*. Norwalk, CT: Appleton-Century-Crofts, 1982.

Westberg, Granger. *Good Grief*. Philadelphia: Fortress Press, 1971.

Williams, Redford and Virginia. *Anger Kills: Seventeen Strategies for Controlling the Hostility That Can Harm Your Health*. New York: Random House, 1993.

Index